THE SPENDOR OF WORSHIP

The Splendor of Worship

Women's Fasts, Rituals, Stories and Art

LAXMI G. TEWARI

MANOHAR
2026

First published 1991
Reprinted 2025, 2026
First eBook edition 2025

ISBN 978-81-85054-94-0 (Hb)
ISBN 978-93-6080-666-8 (ebook)

Published by
Ajay Kumar Jain *for*
Manohar Publishers & Distributors
4753/23 Ansari Road, Daryaganj
New Delhi 110 002

Printed and bound in India

CONTENTS

INTRODUCTION

This book contains folk stories that are an inseparable part of fourteen fasts and festivals celebrated by Kanyakubja Brahman women in the Kanpur district of Uttar Pradesh. The chapters of the book correspond to the festivals[1] and are organized chronologically, according to the Hindu festival cycle; an outline of the customs associated with each festival is followed by the stories told during that festival. Photographs of paintings or sculptures typically made during a festival are given where appropriate.

The fourteen festivals discussed in this book represent only a small number of the fasts and festivals observed by the families of this region. In selecting the festivals for this study, I chose those which are performed solely or mainly by women, and those in which stories and paintings are important.

PURPOSE OF STUDY

India is a land of stories. Some basic religious and mythological stories have been told repeatedly for millennia. Many legends of the ancient Vedic texts reappear, with elaboration, in the Epics and Puranas.[2] Didactic and parabolic fables and stories of the *Pañcatantr-Jātak* type appear first in the original text of the *Pañcatantr*, composed in Kashmir about 200 B.C. (Ryder 1956: 3-4). Elaborations on the *Jātak* tales appear in Buddhaghosa's commentary on the *Dammapad* and the *Avadān*, as well as in Jain literature. Later, more secular stories appear in numerous renditions of the *Brhat-kathā* (including the *Kathāsaritsāgar, Brhatkathāmañjarī,* and *Brhatkathācloksañgrah*) and various versions of the *Vetala-pancavincati, Vikramacharit,* and *Cuksaptali* (Elwin 1944: x).

Old Deccan Days, a collection of stories orally current among the people of India, was published in 1868 (Frere); since then, an ever increasing number of Indian folktales have been printed in and outside India. *A Bibliography of South Asian Folklore* (Kirkland 1966) includes 6,852 books and articles.[3]

During the twentieth century, many studies have been done on Hindu festivals and ceremonies. Some early works gave panoramic views of the whole of India (Buck 1917; Gupte 1919; Sivananda 1947; Underhill 1921), while others concentrated on smaller geographic regions (Lall 1933; Natesa Sastri 1917). One author focused on festivals celebrated by a single caste (Briggs 1920). Later scholars felt that even regional studies were too broad in scope and therefore limited their studies to single villages (Lewis 1965; Marriott 1955; Mathur 1964).

This book is a collection of stories told in the context of women's fasts and festivals. To the best of my knowledge, no similar collection, has been published in the English language. There are a few publications in Hindi (Bharatiya 1974; Gautam 1975), but they were written to codify women's religious practices.[4] Pandey's book (1967) on women's fast stories (from a nearby district) was a significant study. My reason for writing this book was to document tape-recorded stories, with their accompanying artwork, so that this material is available for further study.

METHOD OF RESEARCH

The network of my family's relations directed the initial selection of the families and the geographical area where the research was conducted (an area about fifty kilometers in diameter, in the Kanpur district of Uttar Pradesh—see Map). Most of the interviews took place in the village of Sheoli (about forty-two kilometers from Kanpur city on the Kanpur-Bela Bidhuna Road) or in the city of Kanpur; some stories and paintings were recorded in the cities of Varanasi and Delhi, from women who had moved away from Kanpur after their marriages.

A total of fifteen families were interviewed, often with more than one woman responding; all the informants were Kanyakubja Brahman women. In each interview, I asked for basic family data, tape-recorded the women's repertoire of folk stories told during the fourteen fasts and festivals selected for study, and requested them to draw a folk painting on paper or mold a festival sculpture for me to photograph. Repeated visits were made to each family to record details of ritualistic observances and special food preparation.

During actual fasts, women were generally busy with ritual preparations and did not wish to be distracted by tape-recording. Therefore, with some exceptions, the stories were recorded at

CHINA
JAMMU AND KASHMIR
AFGHANISTAN
TIBET
HIMACHAL PRADESH
PUNJAB
Chandigarh
ARUNACHAL PRADESH
BHUTAN
SIKKIM
PAKISTAN
HARYANA
Delhi (U.T.)
UTTAR PRADESH
NEPAL
RAJASTHAN
ASSAM
NAGALAND
MANIPUR
BIHAR
BANGLA-DESH
MEGHALAYA
MIZORAM
GUJARAT
MADHYA PRADESH
WEST BENGAL
Calcutta
TRIPURA
BURMA
Diu (U.T.)
Daman (U.T.)
MAHARASHTRA
ORISSA
DADRA AND NAGAR HAVELI
Bombay
BAY OF BENGAL
ANDHRA PRADESH
GOA
KARNATAKA
LAKSHADWEEP ISLANDS
Madras
ANDAMAN AND NICOBAR ISLANDS
Pondicherry (U.T.)
TAMIL NADU
KERALA
SRI LANKA

Delhi
UTTAR PRADESH
Ganga River
Sheoli
Kanpur
Yamuna River
Varanasi

other times, not during actual festivals. In a few instances, the situation of telling stories out of context, in the presence of a tape-recorder and several males besides myself, made storytellers self-conscious, with the result that they were often hesitant and shy at the beginning of the storytelling session. For example, my tape of Story No. 36, transliterated and translated word by word, begins as follows:

> Village Sheoli, at the house of Mr. Misra. Mr. Misra, myself(T), Misra's mother (Amma), his wife (Rani), his younger brother's wife, Ramkali (RK) the storyteller, three other neighboring women, and seven children, from age 4 to 12, were present. Time: 10.30 A.M.

T: *Karvā Cauth kī āy, acchā sunāv.*
This is a story of Karvā Cauth? All right, tell us.
RK: *Yākai rahay tau . . . tum bhāgi jāv tau ham kahi den* (laughs).
There once was . . . you go from here, then I will tell.
Amma: *Bhāgi jāy tau phir hiyāñ ko kā kahai?*
If he goes, then what reason is there for telling stories?
T: *Are bhāgai kā, hadd hoi gai.*
Why should I go? That's too much.
Rani: *Jāv batāy dev tab ham bañd kari debai.*
Come on, tell the story. Then I will turn it off (points at the tape-recorder).
T: *Larikai tau āhīñ calau surū karau hāñ nahīñ tau.*
After all, we are all children, so let's begin.
RK: (Laughs loudly.)
Amma: *Hāñ surū karau bhāgi kā jāy* (Some conversation between Amma and the other women).
Let's begin—why should he go?
RK: *Baḍī Līlā hameñ batāvat jāv hameñ dhyān nāhī rahati hai. Dyākhav yākai . . .* (laughs).
O Lila's mother, you refresh my memory, I usually don't remember. Let's see, there once was . . .
T: *Hañsī lev ki batāhī lev. Tumakā to hañsī bahut āvati hai.* (The other women present also begin laughing.)
Either laugh or tell. You laugh too much.
RK: *Yākai rahay . . .* (laughs again).
There once was . . .

One Woman: *Are hasibo to ā jaihai* (laughs).
The laughter will also get recorded.
Rani: *Ājī ke daurā paḍigā hañsī ker* (laughs).
A fit of laughter has taken over grandmother.
T: *Daurā paḍigā lev thoḍā sā piyav, lev ṭhañḍhāī dev Buā kā.*
Buā (father's sister) is having a fit of laughter, so give her some *ṭhañḍhāī* to drink.
Rani: *Ais karau sunau jarā Ājī kā pahile hañsī sunāy dev.*
Listen, let's do this. Let grandmother listen to her laughter first.
T: *Hañsī sunāī tumakā.*
Should I let you hear the laughter?
Amma: *Hāñ hañsī sunāv.*
Yes, let's hear the laughter. (Here I rewind the tape and play it back for her; everyone laughs.)
RK: *Bhāgi jāv sab koī* (laughs; Rani and Amma tell the children to go play outside.)
You all go away from here.
RK: *Kāhe baiṭhā līnhev Līlā kī Ammā* (laughs).
O Lila's mother, why did you make me sit and tell a story?
T: *Ab kaunau nahīñ, sab bhāgi ge, sab bhāgi ge.*
There is no one here now, they're all gone, all gone.
RK: *Acchā bhaī bappā hamār* (laughs).
All right, my father!
T: *Sunāv.*
Please tell.
RK: *Yākai rahay rājā kī beṭī, yākai rahay rājā kī beṭī tau unakā auhāt nahīñ bado rahay. Auhāt nahīñ bado rahay tau ek sanyāsī āo to unake hāth dekhis. Tau kahesi ki hamakā auhāt nahīñ bado hai to kaise kā hoy. To ui kahen ki jāv tum bārā barisai* (Here RK asks Amma if she is telling the story correctly: Amma softly responds, "Yes.") *bārā barisai tum dhobain ker ṭahal karau tau tumakā auhāt milī.* (T: *ṭahal kā?* RK: *ṭahal karau matalab caukā baratan*) *Tau tumakā auhāt milī tau ui jab matalab bārā barasai bhaīñ tau ui kā karaiñ kī sabere khūb rāti ke uṭhaiñ bārā baje au ui jāy unahīñ ke ghare tau sab gadahiyan kai līd pīd sameṭi kai jhāri jhūri kai caukā bāsan sab kari kere ui āy jāyñ. Ui jānai nahīñ pāvaiñ dhobain, jānai nahi pāvaiñ to kahaiñ kī bhai ko ais hai hamare nagra mahiāñ hai dukhī garīb jo kou hamār sab juṭhani dhvāvati hai ā kere aur ham jānay nahīñ pauthin hai. Tau yā bhai ke nā hoy tau bhaī tāḍau sab koi*

jāgau to yekā pakarau. Tau ui kā kann kī bhai sab koi jagāī karin. Jagāī karin ek din unakā pakall linhon. Pakall linhon tau ui māri roīn̐, pāyan mān̐ lapaṭi gaīn̐ ki bhaī hamakā choḍi dev tumhare ke ādamī aihain̐ tau marihain̐ kuṭihain̐ hamakā choḍi dev ab bhai ab ham āj te nā aibe karan. Tau kahin jaun kuch tum kīn hauū taun thīk kīn hauū lekin yau pahile batāv ki kā tum cahatī hau jāhe par tum hamār jūṭhan sametev. Tau kahin kī jaun ham man̐gibe taun tum dyāhav. Tau kanī hān̐ dyāhan. Dyāhan jaun tum man̐gihau. Tau kahin kā man̐gihau. Tau kahin kī ham man̐gibe apane mān̐g kā sen̐dur. Tau ui kahin kī tum to sab kuch mān̐go to jo ui mān̐g kā sen̐dur dīnhon tau unake sab ādamī mari ge. Sab ādamī mari ge to kanī yah to bahut anarth bhā hamare ghar ke to sab ādamī mari ge. To kahin kī o bāīn̐ un̐gariyā kāṭi kere joi o chinik dīnī sab par to sab ādamī thīk hoige. (See the translation of Story No. 36.)

RK: *Aur kuchu?*
Is there anything more?

Amma: *Bas ṭhīk!*
That's enough.

It took approximately one minute and fifteen seconds (out of the total time of three minutes and twenty-five seconds) for Ramkali to begin the story. In contrast, such laughter and need for persuasion were not present at all in the actual worshipping and storytelling which I witnessed.

In translating, the effort has been to adhere to the renderings in Hindi; in Story No. 1, however, where the main character of the story encountered many objects on his journey, I arranged the objects in a corresponding reverse order for the return journey. During subsequent trips to India (summers of 1977 and 1978 and year-long field observations during 1985–86),[5] I returned to Sheoli to re-record a few stories and to verify the translations and local usages of some words and phrases. Out of 137 stories recorded, I selected sixty-nine stories (fifty-five main stories with fourteen variants) for this book. In selecting the main story from a group of similar stories, I chose the one which encompassed the greatest wholeness of the theme. Where variations differed considerably, I included all the significant variations on a story, numbering them 1a, 1b, etc.

All italicised Hindi terminology is included in the glossary.

Where translatable in brief, the Hindi words are translated within parentheses in the text, at their first occurrence.

THE SOCIAL BENEFITS OF THE WOMEN'S DOMESTIC RITUALS AND FOLK ARTS

It is difficult to capture the flavor of Indian daily life without experiencing the richness of the traditions which permeate people's lives. Daily worship of household deities, local shrines, the *tulsī* plant, Mother Earth, the rising sun, God's names, ceremonies of the human life-cycle, festivals of the Hindu year, pilgrimages, visiting sadhus, and folk theater, keep life varied and colorful and raise spirits despite a physically hard existence.

Women have maintained particularly elaborate traditions of worship through fasting, festival celebrations, storytelling, and art. These domestic rituals and folk arts are responsible for transmission of much religious heritage and many cultural norms. Children learn basic customs and religious beliefs through festival stories, paintings, and sculptures; they are socialized in an atmosphere of sharing and cooperation among relatives and neighbors. Girls develop a consciousness of their roles as childbearers and care-givers and of their dependence upon men throughout their lives; boys learn a sense of duty toward their mothers and sisters.

Women derive inspiration from stories of other women's strength in ages past; the festival celebrations also ease the stresses of joint family life, particularly for newly married women, by providing opportunities for them to socialize with women of other households. Through their sincere observance of these festivals, women feel that they assure the overall welfare of their families (see Jacobson 1978:119 and Luschinsky 1962:718). Festival observances help to regulate diet also, for fasting is believed to cleanse the body and festival food preparations break the monotony of villagers' simple diets.

Most important, a sense of communal togetherness is reinforced through exchange of festive foods and expression of values held in common by community members. Children are free to go anywhere in their caste-restricted neighborhood where they are welcomed in every household, given food, discipline, and love, and observe religious practices similar to those in their own homes. Often a festival painting is made in one house and women from several neighboring households come to worship together and tell stories.

Some food is usually reserved for relatives, poor neighbors, and the members of other castes who serve a family; discarded clothing is given on some occasions. Even those of lower caste status may be allowed to observe or participate in the festival, for caste restrictions are more relaxed among women than men (Khare 1976:144). A person's relative status in family or community is also reaffirmed, with the ritual touching of the feet of elders, higher caste members, and other respected persons.

Fasts and festivals encourage sharing and communality among high and low, rich and poor; prosperity and good luck are wished for everyone. Most festival stories end with phrases such as these given below, which bestow auspiciousness indiscriminately on all:

Bhagvān jaise unake din bahure taise sabake bahuraiñ.
(By the grace of God, as their good fortune came, may everyone be blessed similarly.)

Hāre vyopāre sāñjhe āye dīyā bātī,
Sabere āye līpā potī, dupaharī āye jīvā joṭhī.
Dallān bhar bahuriyāñ, okhalī bhar biṭiyāñ;
Nāt lai caḍhau, panāt lai utarau, dhiyā maiyā dīn asīs,
Aur sabakā biṭiyā bahurin kā diñhev suhāg.
(When men work hard all day in business or in the fields, women should purify the house each morning with cowdung paste, prepare the noon meal, and clean the pots.
May such houses be full of daughters-in-law but very few daughters;
May they see the faces of grandsons and great-grandsons.
Thus the mother of daughters bestowed blessings,
May all daughters and daughters-in-law be blessed with matrimony.)

THE FASTS

The women of this area believe that fasting to propitiate specific gods and goddesses assures the health and prosperity of one's family. All fourteen of the festivals represented here are celebrated with definite goals in mind: *Jagannāth*, *Gobardhan*, and *Baḍī Ekādaśī*—for family happiness and prosperity; *Śītalā Aṣṭamī*—to ward off smallpox; *Nāg Pañcamī*—to prevent snake bites; *Bhaiyā*

Dūj—for well-being of brothers; *Bahurā Cauth, Harachaṭh,* and *Avaī Āṭhai*—for protection of sons; *Baragadāhī, Ciraiyā Gaur,* and *Karvā Cauth*—to protect husbands; *Tīj* and *Sakaṭh*—for prosperity and protection of sons and husbands. Except for the Jagannāth and Baḍi Ekādaśī festivals, when both men and women fast and worship, all the rituals mentioned here are performed only by women, some exclusively by married women.[6] (See Table 1.)

The chapters of this book are arranged in the order in which these festivals occur in the *Vikram Samvat* (the Hindu calendar popular in the area of research). In this calendar, the year begins with the new moon of the month of Cait. Each lunar month is divided into two fortnightly halves (*paksh*), each consisting of fifteen lunar days (*tithis*). The fortnight beginning with the night of the new moon (*amāvasyā*) is called the bright half (*śukla paksh* or *sudī*); the fortnight following the night of the full moon (*purṇimāvasyā*) is the dark half (*krishna paksh* or *badī*). (See Table 2.) The timing of a festival is usually calculated according to a numerical day in the bright or dark half of a particular month (*e.g.*, Avaī Āṭhai occurs on the eighth day in the dark half of the month of Kārtik). The names of the lunar months and their Gregorian equivalents are *Cait* (March–April), *Baisākh* (April–May), *Jeṭh* (May–June), *Asāḍh* (June–July), *Sāvan* (July–August), *Bhādau* (August-September), *Kvār* (September–October), *Kārtik* (October–November), *Agahan* (November–December), *Pūs* (December–January), *Māgh* (January–February), and *Phāgun* (February–March).

Almost all the festivals require fasting, followed by specific foods, thereby cleansing the body and then providing appropriate nourishment. Fasting ranges from *nirjalā* (total abstinence from eating or drinking) to specific food which may not or should be eaten. The festival of Harachaṭh, for example, forbids eating *jotā-ann* (plough-produced food), whereas the Ekādaśī fasts prescribe eating of *pūrīs* made of *siṅghāḍā* or *kūṭū* flour, and boiled or fried potatoes. Purity and distinction in cooking ingredients is maintained while preparing the fasting foods. Besides the special food to be eaten by active participants in a fast, many festivals require elaborate preparation of festive food, which is enjoyed by non-fasting members of a family, especially the children. (See the foods for Karvā Cauth described in Khare 1976:138–42.)

TABLE 1

Festival's Name	Time	Deity Worshipped	Purpose	Who Performs it		Folk Art	Fasting
1. Jagannāth Pūjā	Cait 2: Monday	Jagannāth	Family prosperity and protection	Men 26%	Women 39%	Floor painting	Yes
2. Baragadāhī or Sāvitrī Pūjā	Jeṭh 1: Amāvasyā	Banyan tree	Husband's long life	Women 74%		No	Yes
3. Tīj	Sāvan 2:3	Gauri	To obtain a good husband, children and prosperity.	Married & unmarried women 35%		No	Yes
4. Nāg Pañcamī	Sāvan 2:5	Cobra	Family protection	Women 0%*	Children 0%*	Wall painting	No
5. Bahurā Cauth	Bhādau 1:4	Cow with calf	Son's protection	Married women 74%	Widows with sons 17%	Mud sculpture	Yes
6. Harachaṭh	Bhādau 1:6	Goddess Harachaṭh	Son's protection	Married women 96%	Widows with sons 50%	Wall painting	Yes
7. Avaī Āṭhai	Kārtik 1:8	Goddess Avaī Āṭhai	Motherhood and protection of children	Married women 52%		Wall painting	Yes
8. Ciraiyā Gaur	Kārtik 2:1	Bird	To obtain husband's undivided love	Married women 9%		No	Partial

9. Gobardhan	Kārtik 2:1	Krishna	Family prosperity	Women 30%		Widows 17%	Floor sculpture made with cowdung	No
10. Bhaiyā Dūj	Kārtik 2:2	Brother	Brother's welfare	Sisters 61%			Floor painting	Partial
11. Karvā Cauth	Kārtik 2:4	Moon	Husband's long life	Married women 100%			Wall painting	Nirjalā
12. Baḍī Ekādaśī	Kārtik 2:11	Vishnu	Family prosperity and protection	Men 24%	Girls/ married women 48%	Widows 17%	Floor painting	Yes
13. Sakaṭh	Māgh 1:4	Goddess Sakaṭh	Protection of children and prosperity	Married women 87%		Widows 50%	Human figurine made on a wooden board	Yes
14. Śītalā Aṣṭamī or Baseurā	Cait 1:8	Goddess Śītalā	Family protection	Women 74%			No	Yes

* None of the informants mentioned celebrating Annakūṭ, or Nāg Pañcamī, probably because they do not require fasting, although several women told me stories and rituals associated with these festivals. Additionally, Ciraiyā Gaur, Annakūt, and Gobardhan fall on the same day, and Nāg Pañcamī is celebrated mainly by boys and girls, which may account for women neglecting to include them among fasts observed.

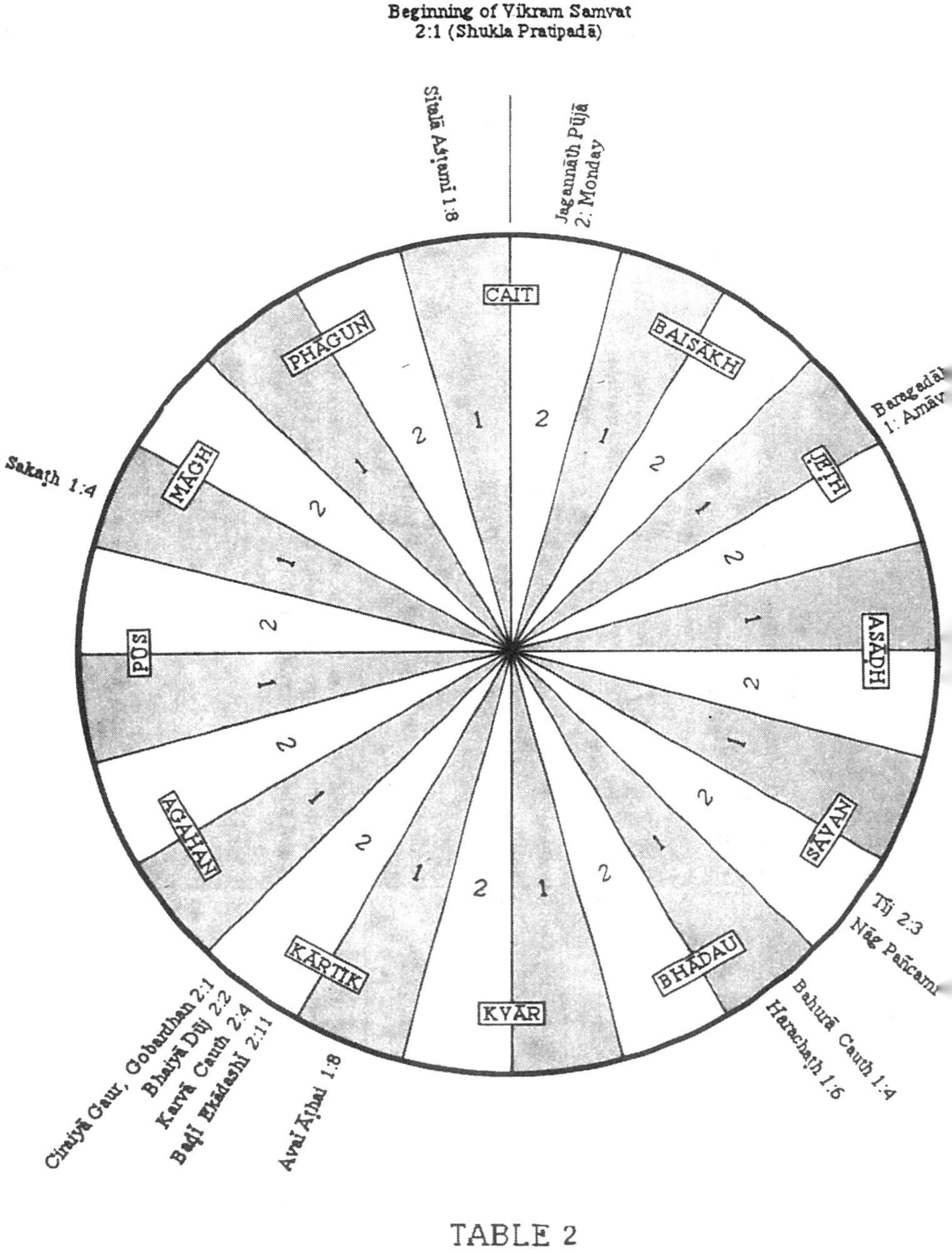
Beginning of Vikram Samvat
2:1 (Shukla Pratipadā)
Sītalā Aṣṭamī 1:8
Jagannāth Pūjā
2: Monday
CAIT
BAISĀKH
JEṬH
ASĀṚH
SĀVAN
BHĀDAU
KVĀR
KĀRTIK
AGAHAN
PŪS
MĀGH
PHĀGUN
Sakaṭh 1:4
Tīj 2:3
Nāg Pañcamī
Bahurā Cauth 1:4
Harachaṭh 1:6
Avaī Āṭhai 1:8
Ciraiyā Caur, Gobardhan 2:1
Bhaiyā Dūj 2:2
Karvā Cauth 2:4
Baḍī Ekādashī 2:11

TABLE 2

Nevertheless, ability to fast is held up as a goal for children to reach for. Mothers suggest to young children, "*Ek ḍāḍh se upāse rahav*" (Fast from one side of your mouth), to inculcate the concept that fasting is good and that they are capable of doing it. Women also claim that fasting helps them concentrate on the reason for worship and facilitates their communication with the deity; they thereby hope to win the deity's favor and all the blessings of a happy life for themselves and other family members. Older girls are subjected to strong psychological pressure to fast and participate in certain rituals, so that they will get good husbands and be prepared for any fasting required at their in-laws' houses. The joint family system makes it almost mandatory for daughters-in-law to fast, in order to make a good impression by following the examples of their mothers-in-law or sisters-in-law; thus if one woman in a household observes a fast, the other women also almost invariably fast.

A general outline of rituals and special food offerings has been given in the introduction to each festival, but no attempt has been made to enumerate all the details of the rituals, for Hindu fasts and festivals "are so numerous, so complex and so easily variable in practice with households, that no claim can be made about covering all the peculiarities" (Khare 1976:125). The basic order of events is that women fast during the day, while preparing any festival foods or paintings required, worship the deity for the festival at the appointed time and in the manner prescribed for that festival, tell the stories associated with it, and then break their fasts.

THE STORIES

The stories in this book are called *vratoṅ kī kathāyeṅ* or *vratoṅ kī kahāniyāṅ* (stories of fasts).[7] Some of the stories explain the origin of a festival, but most of them narrate what has happened to people who did or did not observe the fast in question.

These festival stories portray a morally unambiguous world, which deals out inevitable consequences for actions. The doctrine of *karma* (deeds or works) and the process of transmigration are amply illustrated, for Hindus believe that they reap the rewards and punishments of past actions in their present lives. Through karma, the body of the next life is acquired; a person's character, fortune, social class, and happiness all depend upon previous karma. However, although one has to suffer the consequences of karma accrued from past deeds, right action (*e.g.*, observance of fasts and festivals) can improve a person's lot, either in this lifetime or the next.

These stories also demonstrate some immediate rewards for sincere observance, with punishment befalling those who observe festivals only for material gain. By persistent devotion, it is possible to effect the impossible: many of the stories show magical causality, with dead persons brought back to life by a loved one's total fidelity to rituals (see Stories No. 4, 14, 14a, 16, 16a, 17, 24, 37, and 40) or with characters changing themselves from human to animal forms (see Stories No. 12 and 29).

Worshippers are assured complete access to the deities, who are represented as compassionate, forgiving beings, compelled to grant the wishes of their devotees when faithfully worshipped. Observing a fast is believed to win the good grace of the deity, who then looks after the well-being of the worshipper's entire family. Telling and listening to stories during the fast are considered acts of worship, and thus moral obligations the devotee must fulfil.

Festival times fulfil functions similar to Christian Sunday schools. Children listen eagerly to the festival stories,[8] which cover a great deal of mythology, present strong role models for all family members, and are full of reminders of a person's duties to family, society, and culture.

> An immediate effect is assured, because the tales are not the products of individual experiences and reactions. They are produced, treasured and controlled by the collective working and thinking of the religious community. They thrive on the ever-renewed assent of successive generations. They are effective primarily on a subconscious level, touching intuition, feeling, and imagination. Their details impress themselves on the memory, soak down, and shape the deeper stratifications of the psyche (Zimmer 1946:40).

THE FOLK ART

Many of the fasts and festivals prescribe that women make some type of folk art in order to illustrate the images of the stories. The art usually takes the form of a painting on the wall (for Nāg Pañcamī, Harachaṭh, Karvā Cauth, and Avaī Āṭhai), a painting or object molded of cowdung on the floor (for Gobardhan, Bhaiyā

Dūj, and Baḍī Ekādaśī), or objects shaped out of clay or drawn with *ghī* (clarified butter) on a board (for Bahurā Cauth and Sakaṭh).

For paintings, an area of the wall or floor is first plastered with cowdung or mud; then the painting is made with rice paste (exceptions being that the serpents for Nāg Pañcamī are drawn with coal and the painting of Karvā Cauth is made with many colors, natural or commercial). Dimensions of the paintings range from approximately 2′ × 2′ to 3′ × 3′, except for Bhaiyā Dūj, when the painting may be as large as 5′ × 5′.

Although there is no standard format for making the paintings and women differ in artistic abilities, certain objects are commonly depicted somewhere in each painting. The image of the deity of the festival is drawn in the center of the painting; surrounding it are objects and figures associated with the story of the festival—the sun and moon[9] (top corners), Ganga-Yamuna,[10] savastik, tulsī plant,[11] flowers and birds. Household items, such as mortar and pestle, bucket, child's toy, and comb, are depicted in order to elicit the deity's blessings on those items, which symbolize food, water, children, and matrimony. Lord Ganesh and Hanuman appear in some paintings (see Plates 5, 6, 10, and 12). To show the range of variation commonly seen, I have included three paintings of the Harachaṭh festival (see Plates 3, 4, and 5; Plates 3 and 4 were made by the same informant in consecutive years) and two of the Baḍī Ekādaśī festival (see Plates 11 and 12).

During the worship the painting is marked with *tilak* (a colored mark usually placed on the forehead) and offerings of water and food. Because of these practices and because of the impermanence of the materials used, the paintings begin to peel soon after the worship. "These are artists who rejoice in the act of creation; their paintings are not meant to last, because it is the act of painting, which they consider a prayer, that is important" (Vequaud 1977: 26).

The making of folk art is also viewed as an act of pilgrimage. The preparation of materials and the process of painting or sculpting symbolize the journey to the place of pilgrimage. Worshipping and offering food to the painting or sculpture are acts of *darśan* (auspicious sight) by which a devotee experiences the presence and power of the deity. At the conclusion of the worship, the offerings, supposedly blessed by the deity, are distributed as *prasād* (that which is given out of divine favor).

WOMEN'S ROLES IN THE JOINT FAMILY

During the rituals described in this book, women pray to deities to bless their husbands, brothers, and sons with long lives and prosperity. This is significant, for women are subordinate to and dependent upon male relatives throughout their lives. The *Laws of Manu* (Buhler 1969:195) prescribes:

> In childhood a female must be subject to her father,
> In youth to her husband,
> When her lord is dead to her sons;
> A woman must never be independent.

From the beginning of life, females are considered inferior and burdensome. The birth of a female child is greeted with chagrin, for the family immediately begins to think of their responsibility for finding a husband for her. Not only will they have to pay a sizable dowry and send gifts for every celebration at her in-laws' house, they will forever have to bow down to the members of the family which accepts their daughter.

The birth of a male child, in contrast, is reason for joy and lavish celebration (Tewari 1977). The patrilineal system will be kept intact: the son will support his parents in their old age and the father's funeral rites will be performed satisfactorily. A boy usually remains at home with his parents all his life. His marriage is an occasion for joy, for it means another pair of hands to help with household chores and the possibility of a grandson to carry on the family name.

From early on, a girl is prepared for her duties and the expected hardships at her future in-laws' home. She is taught how to cook, sew, and care for younger siblings and cousins; she is encouraged to participate in fasts and rituals. She is criticized for any behavior which might earn her the reputation of being lazy, disrespectful, or brash. Her marriage is celebrated with rejoicing because her family thus fulfills their main obligation to her, but the actual leave-taking is a time of unrestrained grief. To ease the transition, the bride's first stay at her husband's home is usually brief and is followed by an extended visit to her parents' home. The girl's brother takes on an important significance to her, beyond their close childhood relationship, because he is usually the person sent to her husband's house to bring her home again.

At her in-laws', the new bride is subordinate to her husband, his mother and father, grandparents, older brothers and their wives, sisters, and sometimes other relatives as well.[12] She is often given the hardest work and subjected to many tests of her abilities and character. The most important thing a daughter-in-law can do to elevate her status is to give birth to a son. Despite the injunctions of Manu, grown-up sons continue to respect and obey their mothers; a woman has great influence through her sons. In the event of her husband's death, a woman has three options open to her: (1) remain with her husband's family and raise her sons until they can look after her themselves, (2) go back to her paternal home and be supported by her brothers, or (3) move in with sons who have already grown and settled elsewhere.

A woman's happiness thus depends mainly on her male relatives' prosperity, good health, and kind-heartedness. Women's rituals and fasts are observed in hopes of the fulfillment of these worldly needs and can be divided into the following categories of desire:

1. Affection and well-being of brothers (Bhaiyā Dūj, Nāg Pañcamī).
2. Birth, health, and love of a son (Bahurā Cauth, Harachaṭh, Avaī Āṭhai, Sakaṭh).
3. Matrimony and husband's love (Baragadāhī, Tīj, Ciraiyā Gaur, Karvā Cauth).
4. Family's wealth and auspiciousness (Jagannāth, Annakūṭ, Gobardhan, Baḍi Ekādaśī).
5. Protection from sickness (Śitalā Aṣṭamī).

Most of the rituals described in this book are thus performed for the protection of male relatives.

For the most part, the women interviewed seemed satisfied with the structure of their lives. They regard marriage and bringing up children (preferably sons) as the main purpose of a woman's existence. Whatever status or blessings a woman receives are attributed to her hard work, selflessness, and faithful performance of ritual fasts.

MODERN TRENDS

Many older women, especially in the city of Kanpur, expressed their concern about "modern-educated" daughters-in-law who do not observe these fasts as scrupulously as they did when they were young daughters-in-law. Older women criticize the younger ones for not wearing the traditional *lañhañgā-dupaṭṭā* (long skirt and shawl) for the worship, neglecting to make the folk painting or tell the stories, not making all the prescribed ritualistic food, and making amendments to the fasting requirements by drinking tea. The daughters-in-law, on the other hand, feel that some of these cultural changes of recent years are natural, due to environmental conditions. Many of the daughters-in-law were not given traditional lañhañgā-dupaṭṭā at their weddings and therefore must wear saris instead. Finding time to make a folk painting, prepare ritualistic food, and tell stories seems difficult and pointless when you do not have other relatives to participate or help care for your young children. In cities, making a painting on the wall would ruin the look of a whitewashed or painted house.

The folk traditions of women's ritual storytelling and painting are becoming less and less popular among women of the younger generation, as the effects of modernization spread. The development of technology in cities has created many new jobs, which has lured many young couples away from joint family households. In the absence of in-laws, there is less division of labor: the young wife has to do almost everything herself, for there are no extra hands to help with cooking, child care, laundry, or ritual preparations. Observance of fasts and rituals seems less essential without her mother-in-law and other older women around to criticize and warn her of the dangers of non-observance. Education and a desire to be modern also legislate against superstitious customs; movies, radio, and television now fulfil the entertainment function that festivals once did. Even if a woman has the energy and inclination to observe certain fasts and festivals she may have no female neighbors from her own geographic area to participate in the storytelling and rituals. Thus joint family system has played an important part in the effective transmission of the storytelling and art traditions presented here.

NOTES

1. Throughout the book, when I refer to 'festivals', I mean both fasts and festivals. I use the term 'festival' in the sense of the first meaning given in the

dictionary: 'a time of celebration marked by special observances' (*Webster's Seventh New Collegiate Dictionary*, 1971).

2. The Mahabharata war probably took place about the beginning of the ninth century B.C. (Basham 1959: 39); the epic Mahabharata was composed over a period of some four hundred years, between the second century B.C. and the second century A.D. By the time of writing, the battle was already a legendary event, preserved in the folktales and material records of the ruling tribes (B.A. van Nooten, Introduction to Buck 1973: xiv). 'About the Ramayana's date . . . we accept a period of a few hundred years between 200 B.C. and A.D. 200 as a likely date for its composition . . . . It is safe to say that Valmiki (if he really was the composer) drew upon a number of popular Rama folktakes for his epic . . . .' (B.A. van Nooten, Introduction to Buck 1978: xix).
3. This reference work includes: 'art, ballad, belief, charm, crafts, custom, dance, demonology, drama, epigram, fable, festival, game, gesture, legend, magic, medicine, music, myth, place name, omen, proverb, religion, rhyme, riddle, rite, ritual, song, speech, superstition, tale and witchcraft (Kirkland 1966: viii).' The comprehensive nature of this book perhaps accounts for the large number of listings; additionally, there appear to be some duplications.
4. This includes the publishing of pamphlets and books dealing with fasts and festivals, as well as popular stories. These popular publications are questionable sources, since very little is known about the textual sources, authorship, copyrights, royalties, or publication information (Pritchett 1982:4). It is a flourishing industry, however, some scholars have collected as many as two hundred items on the fasts and festivals of the days of the week and of the year (Wadley 1978a:5).
5. The summer 1978 trip was made possible by a partial travel grant from the American Anthropological Association and a senior fellowship from the American Institute of Indian Studies for 1985-86 field research.
6. I included the Jagannāth festival because of the stories told by women and the Baḍi Ekādaśī festival because of the women's paintings associated with it.
7. The word *kathā* (pl. *kathāyeñ*) and *kahānī* (pl. *kahāniyāñ*) are interchangeable. '*Kathā aur kahānī ekai bāt hai*' (*Kathā* and *kahānī* are the same thing) was the frequent response of women interviewed. A *kathā* is always a religious discourse, while a *kahānī* can be either religious or secular. Another Hindi word used for story is *kissā*, but my informants never used it to denote the story of the fast, because a kissā is always secular.
8. Beyond the women's festivals which are the subject of this book, numerous other festivals are celebrated which involve storytelling, folk drama, and recitation of religious texts.
9. The sun and moon are symbols of chastity and suggest the everlasting union of a devoted wife and her husband. Some myths speak of the sun and moon as brother and sister or as real brothers (see Bedi 1971:15-18).
10. The Ganga is the holiest of all rivers for the Hindus and is believed to wash away all the sins of a person who sees, bathes in, or drinks the sacred water (*darśan, majjan, pān*). In Hindu mythology, Ganga is brought down to earth by way of the severe penances of Bhagirath; Lord Shiva subdues the torrent of Ganga's descent in his matted hair. Each Hindu household keeps some Ganga-water to use in rituals, and to administer to a dying person. The Yamuna is not

as sanctimonious as the Ganga but is considered sacred. She is the sister of Yam, the Gad of Death. In one story (No. 50), told during the festival of Sakaṭh, Ganga and Yamuna are said to be sisters. Ganga-Yamuna are usually represented together as a single symbol in folk painting.

11. The tulsī plant is very sacred to Hindus. Many Hindu households worship the tulsī plant in the evening by placing an oil lamp before it and offering prayers to it. It is believed that evil spirits cannot hover where tulsi is planted and the water which touches its leaves becomes as holy as Ganga-water.
12. A joint family consists of more than one nuclear family living with children under one roof. There is a hierarchy of male and female authority figures, under whose guidance junior members act. The size and nature of joint families differ greatly, but in the area of study, most households interviewed consisted of a grandmother and grandfather, their unmarried daughters and sons, and married sons with wives and children.

I. WORSHIP OF JAGANNĀTH (*JAGDĪSH SWĀMĪ*)

Jagannāth is a fast observed on Monday in the bright half of Cait,[1] by both men and women, to assure prosperity. When a family celebrates on two Mondays, *lapasī* and pūrīs are prepared for the worship the first time; pūrīs, *puā, gojhiyā*, and *gurdhaniyā* are made for the second worship.

A stick of cane, representing Jagannāth, is worshipped. After the worship, the male head of household touches each family member with the stick, to remove all of his or her sins (as in Story No. 1). The following two stories are told by women during the worship. The first story resembles the Krishna-Sudama episode. Pandey (1967:25) explains the background of this festival in detail. He also gives two stories, similar to the ones given here, which are worth comparing.

1. A JOURNEY'S DIVINE REWARD

There was once a Brahman family whose ancestors had faithfully performed the worship of Jagannāth. When the children grew up, however, they didn't bother to worship Jagannāth, and the family as a result became very poor. Eventually the head of the family was forced to go out begging, in order to get food for his family. But it didn't matter how many vegetables, fruits or grains the Brahman brought home; as soon as the Brahman's wife finished preparing it, the food always became one big *roṭī* (bread) and one small roṭī. She used to give the big roṭī to her husband and the small roṭī to their children, while she herself managed to subsist by drinking the water with which she rinsed the kneading bowl.

The Brahman began to wonder what was happening to all the food he brought home, since his wife gave him only one roṭī to eat each day. The next time he brought home a large amount of food, he told his wife, "I will prepare the food today." He cooked a fine meal, but as soon as he invited his wife and children to sit down to eat, the food again became one large roṭī and one small roṭī. The Brahman asked his wife, "Does this happen every day?" "Yes," she replied. He thought for a while and then said, "I must go to the temple of Jagannāth." His wife protested, "How will you survive such a long journey when you have nothing to take with you?"

The Brahman was determined, however, and soon set off on his pilgrimage to Jagannāth. After travelling one day, he camped for the night near a village. Some *banjārās* (grain dealers) who were also camping there gave the Brahman some bread dough, so that he could prepare some food for himself. The poor Brahman thought of his family with guilt, "I have plenty of food to eat tonight, but my wife and children probably have nothing." He learned that a milkmaid was going to his village, so he gave her half of his bread dough to take to his wife.

When the milkmaid reached the village, she noticed that the dough had turned to solid gold and decided to keep it for herself. As a result, all the animals at her house started to die. When she reached home, her mother-in-law questioned her, "What have you done today, to cause this misfortune?" The milkmaid confessed what had happened, and her mother-in-law ordered her to take the gold to the Brahman's wife immediately. As soon as the milkmaid returned the gold, all the animals came back to life.

Meanwhile, the Brahman continued on his journey. On the way, he met an elephant who was trying to move this way and that, but couldn't seem to move away from one spot. "Where are you going?" asked the elephant. "To see Jagannāth," replied the Brahman. "Please offer my prayers also, and ask Jagannāth what sin I have committed, that I am tied to this lock of hair," begged the elephant. The Brahman promised to ask Jagannāth and continued on his way.

Soon the Brahman met a cow and a calf who were both crying. "Where are you going?" asked the cow. "To see Jagannāth," replied the Brahman. "Oh!" pleaded the unhappy cow, "please offer my prayers also, and ask Jagannāth what sin I have committed, that my calf cannot take my milk from me." The Brahman promised to ask Jagannāth and continued on his way.

After a while the Brahman saw two ponds which stretched towards each other. "Where are you going?" they asked. "To see Jagannāth," replied the Brahman. "Please offer our prayers also," the ponds requested, "and ask Jagannāth what sins we have committed, that we both fill up during the rainy season, but never meet." The Brahman promised to ask Jagannāth and continued on his way.

Next the Brahman met a she-cobra, writhing from the heat on the road. "Where are you going?" she asked. "To see Jagannāth," replied the Brahman. "Please offer my prayers also," moaned the she-cobra, "and ask Jagannāth what sin I have committed, that I suffer day and night in this hot dirt and am unable to move into the shade." The Brahman promised to ask Jagannāth and continued on his way.

Before long, the Brahman met a man who was carrying a hot *berausī* (bowl of hot coals) on his head. "Where are you going?" he asked. "To see Jagannāth," replied the Brahman. "Please offer my prayers also," the man beseeched, "and ask Jagannāth what sin I have committed, that I am compelled to carry this hot berausī on my head day and night and can never put it down." The Brahman promised to ask Jagannāth and continued on his way.

Further on, the Brahman saw a woman sitting on a *maciyā* (sitting stool). "Where are you going?" she asked. "To see Jagannāth," replied the Brahman. "Please offer my prayers also," she said, "and ask Jagannāth what sin I have committed, that I must sit on this maciyā day and night and am unable to push it away from me." The Brahman promised to ask Jagannāth and continued on his way.

By then the Brahman was nearing the temple of Jagannāth. As he approached, he met another Brahman (actually, the god Jagannāth in disguise).

"Where are you going?" asked the other Brahman.

"To see Jagannāth," replied the Brahman.

"The dangers are many," warned the other Brahman, testing him. "If you become blind, how will you get there?"

"I will feel my way along," replied the Brahman.

"If you become lame, too, how will you get there?" asked the other.

"I will crawl along," replied the Brahman.

"All right," the other Brahman challenged him, "if you jump into this fire, I will know that you are truly determined to reach Jagannāth's temple."

The Brahman immediately stepped forward toward the fire, but the other Brahman stopped him, saying, "How would you like to see the god Jagannāth right here?"

"I am not that lucky," replied the Brahman. "Let me go on."

"No," said the other Brahman. "Close your eyes for a minute."

The Brahman did as he was bidden; when he opened his eyes, he saw the god Jagannāth standing before him in all his glory.

The Brahman prostrated himself before Jagannāth and gave him the rice he had brought from home as an offering. Jagannāth began to eat the rice, but after he had eatern two mouthfuls, his wife Rukmani appeared. "You have already given the Brahman two worlds by eating his rice," she warned. "Don't give me away also." Jagannāth stopped eating the rice, and from then on the Brahman enjoyed many luxuries at the temple. After a while, he began to feel guilty for enjoying himself while his family might be suffering in his absence.

In the meantime, Jagannāth had ordered Visvakarma to transform the Brahman's hut into a mansion and provide his family with all the luxuries of life. At home, the Brahman's wife was astonished, but merely told Visvakarma not to move the tulsī plant. The Brahman did not know that this was happening at his home and asked Jagannāth for permission to leave. "Stay a while longer," said Jagannāth. "Please, Lord," begged the worried Brahman, "I must go home and take care of my poor family." Reluctantly, Jagannāth said, "All right, you may go home now."

After the Brahman had travelled a short distance, he became deaf. He returned quickly to Jagannāth and complained, "I gained nothing by coming here, and on top of that, I have become deaf." "Did you have any messages to give me?" asked Jagannāth. The Brahman suddenly remembered everyone he had met on the way and realized that he had forgotten to ask Jagannāth any of the questions he had promised to ask. "Tell me everything," said Jagannāth.

"What sin did the elephant commit, that he is tied to a lock of hair and cannot move from that spot?" asked the Brahman. Jagannāth answered, "The elephant was a barber in his previous life, but he never cleaned his comb. Touch the elephant with the cane I gave you and the lock of hair will fall away from him."

"What sin did the cow commit, that she cannot give her milk to her calf?" asked the Brahman. Jagannāth answered, "The cow was a *ṭonahinī* (enchantress) in her previous life. Go and milk her five times in your name and five times in my name and she will be able to nurse her calf."

"What sins did the two ponds commit, that they can never join each other, even after heavy rains?" asked the Brahman. Jagannāth answered, "The two ponds were *jeṭhānī* (husband's elder brother's wife) and *devarānī* (husband's younger brother's wife) in their previous lives, but they fought too much. Drink five handfuls of water in your name and five handfuls of water in my name from each pond, and they will flow together."

"What sin did the she-cobra commit, that she suffers in the hot dirt?" asked the Brahman. Jagannāth answered, "In her previous life she had some grain parched, but she did not pay the grain-parcher for it. Touch her with the cane I gave you and she will be able to move out of the sun."

"What sin did the man commit, that he cannot take the hot berausī off his head?" asked the Brahman. Jagannāth answered, "In his previous life he once met a man carrying a big load on his head, but refused to help the man put his load down. Touch him with the cane I gave you and he will be able to put the berausī down."

"What sin did the woman commit, that she is stuck to the maciyā that she sits upon?" asked the Brahman. Jagannāth answered, "The woman did not respect her *sasur* (father-in-law) and *jeṭh* (husband's elder brother) in her previous life; she sat upon the maciyā in front of them. Touch her with the cane I gave you and the maciyā will come unglued."

After the Brahman asked all these questions, his hearing was restored. Still he wondered why Jagannāth had not given him anything to take home. Jagannāth told him, "Arrange a great feast on Monday and tell everyone to worship Jagannāth." The Brahman promised to do so and set off on his homeward journey once again. On the way the Brahman told all the sinners the reasons for their curses and released them according to Jagannāth's instructions.

When the Brahman reached his village, he couldn't find his cottage anywhere, so he began to call out the names of his wife and children. When his wife heard his voice, she told her son to go find his father. The boy answered disrespectfully, "Let him shout. Since he has been gone, we have eaten well and live nicely." His mother told him and all the other children, "All of our good fortune is only because of your father's pilgrimage to Jagannāth. Go and bring him home with the respect he is due." The son went out and found his father, but the Brahman refused to come in, saying, "This is not my home."[2]

The Brahman then went to his elder daughter's house, where his granddaughter was playing outside. It was Monday, so he asked her to go inside and tell her mother, "Your father has come and is asking for wheat and *guḍ* (raw sugar) so that he can worship Jagannāth before he eats." The granddaughter gave the message to her mother, but she answered, "Let him sit there! He always comes and asks for something."

Upon hearing this, the Brahman decided to go to his younger daughter's house. On his way through the *khalihān* (threshing area), he met a lady who lived there. "Please give me some wheat and guḍ for the worship of Jagannāth," he begged, but she refused. As soon as the Brahman left, the whole khalihān caught fire.

Finally the Brahman reached his younger daughter's house and asked for the items necessary for Jagannāth's worship. This daughter was very poor and had nothing in her house, but she went to the merchant's shop and left her son there with the merchant's servant, in return for some wheat and guḍ. When she gave them to her father, he told her to bathe, put on frêsh clothes, and come listen to the story of Jagannāth. She hesitated, because the only sari she owned was the one she was wearing. Upon her father's insistence, however, she went and looked in her closet and was astounded to find it full of beautiful new clothes. She bathed quickly, put on one of the new saris, and came to participate in the worship. When her father finished worshipping Jagannāth, he gave her some prasād and left for home. The daughter ate some of the prasād and put some aside to give to her son later.

In the meantime, the merchant returned to his shop and asked his servant, "Who is this boy?" The servant answered, "A Brahman lady came to buy wheat and guḍ for the worship of Jagannāth, but she didn't have any money, so she left her son here." The merchant immediately ordered the servant to take the boy back to his mother. When the boy arrived home, his mother gave him his share of the prasād, but he was unable to eat it. "It is too hard," he complained. His mother came and saw that the praŝad had turned to gold.

Returning home through the khalihān, the Brahman was stopped by the lady he had asked for wheat and guḍ. "What evil magic did you perform, to make the khalihān burn down?" she challenged him. He replied, "I did nothing. The god Jagannāth made this happen because of your refusal."

When the Brahman reached home, he sent invitations for both of his married daughters to attend a big feast in honor of Jagannāth, to be held the following Monday. He spent the entire week making preparations. When the feast day came, all of the invitees showed up, including the elder daughter who had scorned her father. When she tried to enter her father's house, however, she was unable to. Finally her father prayed to Jagannāth, "Please let my daughter enter." The daughter walked in and sat down, but when she tried to eat, the pūrīs turned into leaves and the guḍ into ashes. Again the Brahman prayed to Jagannāth, "Please forgive my daughter for her pride." Then everything returned to normal and everyone lived in peace and happiness.[3] (MAHADEVI—70—KANPUR CITY)

2. THE SACRED TANK

There once lived an old woman who was sad because her son had been abroad for twelve years. One day she went to bathe in a tank next to the temple of Somnath. A group of girls was bathing on one side of the tank and a group of boys on the other side. All of the boys were deformed and suffering from leprosy; before they bathed, they prayed to the god Somnath, "If our afflictions are cured, we will offer you golden pots in thanks." As soon as they entered the water, their bodies became beautiful.

The boys splashed about in joy, but the old woman thought they were laughing at her. "Don't make fun of me! Can't you see that I'm an old woman?" she shouted at them. "Oh, mother, don't be angry," one of the boys apologized, "we were not laughing at you. We were just laughing in happiness, because our bodies have been made straight and healthy again." "How did that happen?" queried the old woman. The boy answered, "We prayed to Somnath before bathing and promised to offer him golden pots if he cured us. Look at the girls on the other side, too, how happy they are! They also prayed to Somnath before bathing, promising him golden pots if they were blessed with good husbands. They too have had their wishes fulfilled."

Upon hearing this, the old woman thought, "If Somnath is so powerful, I will pray to him also." Standing on the edge of the tank, she prayed, "Oh, Somnath, I will give you a golden pot, if my son, who has been away for twelve years, returns to live with me." Then she bathed in the tank and returned home to find her son waiting outside the house. The old woman was overjoyed and told him what she had seen at the tank and how she had prayed for his return. "I must go and offer a golden pot to Somnath immediately," she said.

"Wait, mother," her son said, "don't offer the pot yet. I will offer it after I am married." His marriage was soon arranged and he lived happily with his wife. "Why are you so happy?" asked his wife one day. "I rejoice at the power of the god Somnath," her husband answered. "Lepers prayed to him and were blessed with healthy bodies, girls prayed to him and were blessed with good husbands, my mother prayed to him and I returned from abroad, and I prayed to him and got you."

His wife said, "Whatever you offered, I also will offer if I am blessed with a son." Nine months later, she gave birth to a son and was very happy. When the child grew older, he asked his mother, "Why are you so happy?" She answered, "I am happy because of the power of god Somnath." And she told her child how everyone's prayers had been answered, from the lepers to herself. Upon hearing this, the child said, "Don't offer a golden pot yet. I will offer one if I am blessed with a kingdom." In time, the child became a king and offered many golden pots to the god Somnath.[4]
(PHOOLMATI—81—SHEOLI)

NOTES

1. Data from informants differed: some celebrated on the first Monday, others on both Mondays in the bright half; some celebrated on the first Monday of each half of the month.
2. Another informant, Phoolmati—81—Sheoli, told a similar story; when the Brahman sees how his home has changed, he exclaims:

Hiyāñ hatī morī ṭūṭī maḍaiyā,	My broken hut was here,
Kañcan mahal khaḍe.	Where this golden palace stands.
Sudāmā mañdir dekh dare.	Sudama is frightened by the sight of the palace.
'Hiyāñ hatī morī būcī gagariyā,	My broken pot was here,
Sone ke kalas dhare.	Where golden pots sit now.
Hiyāñ hatī morī bhūkhī Brāhmanī,	My hungry wife was here,
Suñdar nāri khaḍī.	Where a beautiful woman is standing.

Sudāmā mandir dekh dare.	Sudama is frightened by the sight of the palace.

3. See Pandey 1967:38; "The Hero on Pilgrimage" in Elwin 1944:279–90; and "Giant Ramhah and Goddess Synshar" in Bareh 1971:15–25.
4. See Pandey 1967:46; Bedi 1971:138; "Amritsar—The Legend of the Sacred Tank" in *North Indian Notes and Queries*, 3 (9):162 (December 1893).

II. BARAGADĀHĪ (*SĀVITRĪ PŪJĀ*)

Baragadāhī is a festival performed by married women on the last day of the dark half of Jeth, for the prosperity and long lives of their husbands. According to Pandit Harihar Shastri,[1] this fast is supposed to last for three days; if a woman cannot observe it for three days, she must fast at least one day. Until she has worshipped the *baragad* (banyan) tree, she is not supposed to eat or drink anything, not even water.

Women put on their best ornaments and decorate their feet with *mahāvar* (a red dye). They go outside to a baragad tree for the worship (or make a small tree in their homes by planting a few baragad twigs in a clay pot). Each woman carries a plate with materials for the worship. First, the women sprinkle water on the tree, then they make a design of two or five concentric circles on the ground, using *aipan* (thin rice paste). They place five clumps of clay (symbolizing Gauri) on top of the design, sprinkle water twice over this, and then dab *seṅdur* (red powder) three times on the central clump. Each woman applies aipan to the trunk of the tree twelve times and wraps thread around the tree twelve times. She offers a cantaloupe, twelve split chickpeas (soaked), five baragad buds, and pūrīs to the tree, placing a *janeū* (the sacred thread) on top. All the women walk around the tree twelve times, dropping one grain of split chickpea each time. Each woman breaks a leaf bud of the tree into twelve pieces and swallows them without chewing, along with twelve grains of split chikpeas. She places a janeū over another woman's neck, saying, "Your husband sent this." A ghī lamp is burned by the group and each woman embraces the tree seven times, alternating left and right sides. She touches the feet of her husband and other respected family members and then eats her prasād.[2]

3. WHY WOMEN WORSHIP THE BANYAN TREE

Long ago, it was a custom that women gave their husbands yellow rice on the night before the Baragadāhī amāvasyā, telling them,

"Tomorrow we will fast for you." The men put the rice in the *ghanaucī* (a raised platform for water pots), because it was a pure place. In the morning, the women applied *ubṭan* (a paste used to smear the body) to their husband's bodies and bathed them. They gave the men new janeū, performed the *āratī* on them, offered them the special foods made for the occasion, and gave them presents.

One year, for some reason, a woman was not able to perform the Baragadāhī fast, so her husband hit her. Angrily, the woman responded, "I have performed this fast faithfully for you for many years, yet because I cannot do it this one year, you hit me. I will not worship you anymore, but will worship the baragad tree instead." Thus the tradition of worshipping the baragad tree began. (BUDDHAMATI—48—SHEOLI)

4. SĀVITRĪ AND SATYAVĀN

Once there lived a girl named Sāvitrī, who was very dear to her father, the king. When she reached a marriageable age, her father told her to go out and select the groom of her choice. She traveled far and wide looking for a man who suited her, but to no avail. She had almost given up, when she saw Satyavān panting and fell in love with him immediately. She determined to marry him and no one else. The ministers who had accompanied her on the trip told this to the king when they returned.

In the meantime, the sage Narad came to the court and told the king that Satyavān had but one more year to live. The king tried to dissuade his daughter from marrying Satyavān, but she insisted, "I have accepted Satyavān as my husband in my heart. I don't care if he lives for only one year, or even for just one day. I will not marry any other man."

Sāvitrī was therefore married to Satyavān and went to live with her blind in-laws in the forest. Each day Satyavān used to go to the forest to collect wood for the fire and fruit for their meals. Sāvitrī counted the days carefully as they passed. On the last day of the year, she begged her husband to take her to the forest with him. Satyavān tried to convince her that it would be too hard for her in the forest and she should stay at home to care for his parents. Sāvitrī insisted, however, and at last her husband agreed to let her accompany him.

While Satyavān was cutting wood in the forest, he was suddenly afflicted with a severe headache. Sāvitrī told him to come down from the tree and made him lie down and rest his head in her lap. Soon Satyavān was dead. Dharm-raj (Yam) came to take Satyavān's soul away, but Sāvitrī followed him. When Yam looked behind him and saw Sāvitrī following him, he told her to return home. "What is the use of returning without my husband?" she replied. Yam said, "Because of your devotion, you may ask me for anything except your husband." Sāvitrī requested, "I would like to have one hundred sons." Without thinking, Yam said, "Your desire shall be granted."

Yam continued on with Satyavān's soul, but when he looked behind him again, he realized that Sāvitrī was still following him. "I have given you one boon and now you should return home. I will grant you another boon, however, except for the return of your husband," offered Yam. "Cure my in-laws' blindness," asked Sāvitrī. "Your desire shall be granted," said Yam, continuing on his way with Satyavān's soul.

When Yam looked back again, he saw Sāvitrī quietly walking behind him. "Ask one more boon, excepting your husband's life, then return home," he ordered. Sāvitrī requested, "Restore my father-in-law's rightful kingdom to him, so that I will have the means to take care of my one hundred sons." "Granted!" replied Yam, who was getting annoyed with Sāvitrī. "Go home now!" He continued on his way with Satyavān's soul.

Once again Yam turned around; there was Sāvitrī right behind him. "Go no further!" he thundered. "I have granted you three boons and can offer no more." Sāvitrī reasoned with him, "You have promised me one hundred sons, but you are taking my husband away from me. I am a pious and dedicated woman. Do you want me to become unchaste? How can I have one hundred sons without my husband?" Hearing this, Yam realized his mistake and bowed to Sāvitrī for her devotion. Then he released Satyavān's soul and told Sāvitrī to return to the spot where his body lay. As soon as Sāvitrī put Satyavān's head on her lap again, he came back to life, rubbing his eyes and saying, "I slept a very long time today. We should return home to my parents immediately."

In the meantime, Satyavān's parents had regained their sight and their kingdom, but they worried about their son and daughter-in-law, thinking, "Why have they left us alone?" Sāvitrī and

Satyavān returned late in the evening, prostrated before the old couple, and related the story of what had happened.

Since then the worship of *Vaṭ Sāvitrī* has been performed by Hindu women.[3] (BHAGWATI PANDEY—57—KANPUR CITY).

NOTES

1. Interview with Pandit Harihar Shastri of Kanpur city, summer 1975.
2. See also Khare 1976:127–29.
3. See "Savitri" in Devee 1919:82–96; Gupte 1919:246; "Savitri, The Indian Alcestis" in Nivedita 1975:51; Sita 1970: 46; Lall 1933:92; and Ross 1914:71. Pandit Harihar Shastri of Kanpur city also told a similar story.

III. TĪJ

Sāvan, the fifth month of the Hindu year, is a great month for festivals. After the burning hot summer months, the sky is full of dark clouds, announcing the coming of the monsoon season, to everyone's relief. The air is full of sweet, earthy odors and everyone is happy. This happiness begins the chain of festivals. There is a saying that the Tīj festival comes and sows the seeds of festivals; Holi comes and takes away the festivals in her shawl (Lewis 1965: 205).

Tīj (also known as *Haritālikā*) is performed on the third day of the bright half of Sāvan (or Bhādau). Tīj in Sāvan marks the beginning of the swinging season. A swing is hung inside the house or outside on the trees; swinging and singing are enjoyed most by the children and women. Songs sung at this time are called *Kajarī* or *Kajalī* (a type of song sung in the rainy season), *Sāvan* (a song type), and *Jhūlā ke Gīt* (swinging songs). Both married and unmarried women fast on this day and worship the Goddess Parvati, in order to get (keep for life) a good husband, prosperity, and children.

5. PARVATI'S PERSISTENCE

In one incarnation, Parvati was the daughter of King Daksha and married Shankar*ji*, against the wishes of her father. One time, the king went to invite Shankar*ji* to a great sacrifice. Shankar*ji* was deep in meditation and did not get up to greet his father-in-law. The king took this as an insult, thinking, "The whole world pays respect to me, but my own son-in-law is arrogant." King Daksha therefore left without inviting Shankar*ji*. When Parvati learned of the sacrifice, she wanted to go, but Shankar*ji* told her, "You should not go where you are not invited." Parvati argued, "One can go to his or her Guru's house or father's house without invitation."

Parvati insisted on going to the sacrifice. Shankar*ji* refused to go with her, but sent Kagabhusundi to accompany her. When Parvati arrived at her father's house, no one would talk to her, much less welcome her. Parvati saw that shares of the sacrifice were being given to all the sons-in-law, but nothing had been reserved for Shankar*ji*. In sadness and shame, Parvati died on the spot.

Kagabhusundi returned to Shankar*ji* and reported what had transpired. Shankar*ji* angrily plucked a hair out of his matted locks and threw it down upon the ground, whereupon a demon immediately sprung up. "Go to King Daksha's palace, kill everyone there, and destroy the sacrifice!" Shankar*ji* ordered. The demon broke the limbs of everyone assembled at the sacrifice, cut off King Daksha's head, and threw it into the sacrificial fire. Shankar*ji* arrived soon after and sorrowfully cremated Parvati's body.

In her next lifetime, Parvati was born to King Himancal. Knowing that Parvati had vowed to be wedded to Shankar*ji* whenever she was reborn, Narad*ji* told the king that her marriage to Shankar*ji* was inevitable. This displeased the king, for he thought, "Shankar*ji* is only a sadhu. He does nothing but meditate all day long. My daughter deserves to be married to a rich king." When Parvati heard this, she left home with a maidservant and went to the forest to do penance. When it rained, Parvati stood out in the open. When the sun shown down on the hottest days, Parvati burned fires all around herself to make it even hotter. In this manner, Parvati performed twelve years of penance.

One day, Shankar*ji* came to test Parvati. "Whose daughter are you?" he asked. Parvati's maidservant answered for her, "She is the daughter of King Himancal and is doing penance because she wants to marry Shankar*ji*, although her father wants her to marry a rich king." Shankar*ji* deprecated himself, saying, "Why does she want to marry Shankar*ji*? He does not have a good home, he has nothing to ride but a bull, and all he does is meditate and wander here and there. He is good for nothing!" Parvati refused to listen to him, however, so he finally left, unable to dissuade her from her vow.

In the meantime, sage Narad had told King Himancal of his daughter's whereabouts and her determination to marry Shankar*ji*. The king acknowledged his defeat and sent for Parvati, promising to arrange the marriage she desired so greatly. The king approached Shankar*ji*, offering his daughter's hand to him, and Parvati and Shankar*ji* were married once again.

Parvati left home to do her penance on the third day of the

bright half of Bhādau; that is why this festival is also called Haritālikā.[1] (BHAGWATI PANDEY—57—KANPUR CITY).

NOTE

1. See "Sati" in Devee (1919: 1–16; "Haritalika and Kokila Vrata" in Gupte 1919; "Sati, The Perfect Wife" and "The Tale of Uma Haimavati" in Nivedita 1975: 33; Sita 1970: 81; and Dimmitt 1978: 157–79.

IV. NĀG PAÑCAMĪ

Nāg Pañcamī, also known as *Guḍiyā* (doll) or *Guḍiyā kā Melā* (Festival of Dolls), is celebrated on the fifth day of the bright half of Sāvan.

Women fast on this day. They paint a section of the wall white with rice paste and draw snakes with lampblack (see Plate 1). Then they worship this painting with milk and *ghughari* (boiled wheat and chickpeas). During the worship, women tell stories and pray for their families and brothers. Snake charmers tour the neighborhoods, showing their cobras in return for offerings of milk, festive food, and a few coins. Girls and married women receive gifts of bangles, hair tassels, and saris from the parents. Girls go to the fair with their dolls, which they drop at places set up by boys who beat the dolls. Two stories (No. 6a and 8) give reasons for the custom of beating the dolls. In Kanpur city, the beating is done by lower-caste boys, who are given some coins and ghugharī. Coconut, *misrī* (sugar-candy), and ghugharī are eaten by everyone on this day. Wrestling matches are a must.

Snake worship is popular in different forms throughout India. In the area of study, people believe that a cobra will not bite a person if he says, "*Ham bhaine tum māmā*" (I am your nephew and you are my maternal uncle). The festival of Nāg Pañcamī represents a contract between human beings and the poisonous snakes which are forced out of their holes by the rain and seek shelter in the dry areas of mud houses and barns. Worshipping the snakes and offering them milk is thus a sign of goodwill.

The social significance of this festival is that it is customary to bring newly married girls back to their paternal homes to stay for the whole month of Sāvan. Many folk songs express girls' eagerness for their brothers to come and fetch them. At home they enjoy swinging and singing with their old friends. The air is filled with sweet melodies and the giggling chatter of young women.

6. COBRA-BROTHER'S REVENGE TRANSCENDED

Once there was a girl who was very badly treated by her stepmother and stepbrother. One day when the girl's father was out, her stepmother threw her out of the house. Weeping, she went to the forest and lay down near a snake's hole. Putting her hand down into the hole, she cried, loudly, "Bite me, snake, so that I can die." Two or three days passed, but she was not bitten.

The hole was inhabited by a cobra couple who were suffering for their wrongdoings as human beings in previous lifetimes. The she-cobra listened to the girl's pitiful cries and her heart went out to her. Finally, she could control herself no longer and said to her mate, "That poor girl is crying so much I can't bear it. Why don't we adopt her as our own daughter?" The cobra agreed and they brought the girl into their home.

The girl lived there happily for some time. She was permitted to wander around the whole house, with the exception of one room, which the she-cobra warned her never to enter. One day when the cobra couple was out, the girl's curiosity got the better of her and she opened the door to the forbidden room. It seemed to be empty, except for a big earthen pot, but when she lifted the lid to look inside, seven baby cobras crawled out of the pot. Hastily, she shoved them back into the pot and clamped the lid on. In doing so, the youngest cobra's tail got caught on the rim and was cut off. The girl shamefacedly told her snake mother what she had done, but was readily forgiven. Some time later the cobra couple arranged her marriage and sent her off to her husband's home.

Once the girl had left, the cobra couple let the baby cobras loose to romp and play together. The older ones began to tease the youngest brother, calling him "snake without a tail." One day he got so angry that he went to his mother and asked her how his tail had gotten cut off. She tried to dissuade him, but he insisted on knowing the story. Finally she told him, "One day your human sister opened the pot in which you and your brothers were growing. In her fright, she put the lid back on in a hurry; your tail got caught on the rim and was cut off." Upon hearing this incident, the angry young cobra determined to find his human sister and take revenge by biting her.

By chance, it was Nāg Pañcamī. The young married girl felt very sad that she didn't have any brothers to worship that day, since her stepbrother was cruel and her seven snake-brothers didn't know her. She wanted to perform the worship anyway, so she drew pictures of her seven snake-brothers on the wall and worshipped them.

When the young cobra arrived at her house, he saw his sister crying and performing the worship of Nāg Pañcamī, praying, "May my snake-brother without a tail live long and be prosperous." Repenting for his intended action, the snake crawled in front of her and said, "Don't be sad; your brother has come. Apply tilak." Thus both brother and sister were happy.[1] (GEETA TIWARI—26—KANPUR CITY).

6a. VARIATION ON STORY NO. 6

The story is similar to the preceding one, except that it is the girl's in-laws who throw her out and the cobra couple tell her that they are her godparents. When she opens the forbidden door (the 7th room of the house), she crushes many baby snakes and eggs. The godfather snake takes her back to her husband's home, sending much wealth and clothing with her. All of the young snakes go to her house, to take revenge for their broken tails, but they hear her praying, "*Nāg baḍhai nāganiyā bāḍhai, bāḍhai rāj chamāsī. Dūdh mūdh mor bhaiyā bāḍhai, jin puraī mor āsī.*" (May the cobra couple multiply. May their kingdom expand. May my brothers with broken tails prosper, because they fulfilled my wishes.) The snakes then return home and make dolls that they beat instead of their godsister. Since that time, people have beaten dolls and worshipped snakes on this day. (RANI MISRA—34—DELHI).

7. COBRA-BROTHER TO THE RESCUE

There was once a young married girl whose brother did not come to take her to her parents' home on Nāg Pañcamī. Her mother-in-law and husband's elder brother's wife taunted her, saying, "Poor girl! You don't have a brother or a brother's wife." Weeping bitterly, the girl went to the field to cut grass. A cobra slid up and asked why she was crying so hard. "My mother-in-law and husband's elder brother's wife are teasing me because my brother didn't come to take me home on Nāg Pañcamī," sobbed the girl. "Don't cry," soothed the cobra. "Tell your in-laws that your snake-brother will come to take you home."

Naturally, when the girl told this to her in-laws, they laughed at her. As promised, however, the cobra appeared in human form, bearing a cartload of gifts for the girl's in-laws. He took the girl to *Nāglok* (the abode of snakes) and provided her with food and luxuries. Although the girl didn't know how to speak to the other snakes, she enjoyed living there. When the prescribed month had passed, the cobra returned her to her in-laws' home, with all the customary presents.

Thus the girl's mother-in-law and husband's elder brother's wife came to respect her.[2] (BHAGWATI SHUKLA—54—VARANASI).

8. WHY DOLLS ARE BEATEN ON NĀG PAÑCAMĪ

A king was out hunting one day when he came upon a sage deep in meditation in the forest. As a joke, the king put a dead snake around the sage's neck. The sage angrily cursed the king, saying that he would die from a snake bite. The king consulted his counsel of elders and priests who told him that he could not avoid the snake's bite, but he could attain *moksh* (liberation) by listening to the *Srimad Bhagavat.* Realizing his death was imminent, the king arranged for the *Srimad Bhagavat* to be recited for seven days. At the end of the reading, the priest put a garland around the king's head; the garland turned into a snake and bit the king, and the king died.

When the king's son assumed the throne, he thought, "My father was very powerful, yet he died of a snake bite." He consulted the priests and decided to perform a snake sacrifice. As soon as the sacrifice began, snakes began to fall on the fire from every direction. The thousand-hooded snake feared for his life, so he asked Mahadev for help. Mahadev said he couldn't help him, so the snake went to Indra. He in turn said he could not help. In desperation, the serpent wrapped himself around Indra's throne. When the priest poured *āhuti* (oblations) on the sacrificial fire, Indra's throne began to move toward the fire. This frightened Indra, and he begged the king's son and the priests to have pity on him and on the snake who was seeking his protection. The king's son bargained, "I will spare this snake only if he becomes a Brahman and promises that he will never assume his snake form again."

The snake agreed and began to live as a Brahman. In time, he was married and had a son. One day his wife asked him to take care of the baby while she went to fetch water. Feeling bored, the Brahman thought to himself, "I wonder if I can change back into a snake again. No one will see me." He transformed himself into a snake and rose up next to his son, with his hood spread out. In the meantime, his wife came back and saw the snake hovering over her son. Quickly, the snake changed back into a Brahman again. The wife asked, "Where were you? There was a snake right next to our son." He protested, "I was here watching the baby the whole time and I didn't see a snake. You are mistaken." The wife insisted, however, so he finally had to tell her how he was transformed from a snake into a Brahman. "Don't tell anyone this story," he warned, "or you will lose your husband."

The wife kept the secret as long as she could. One day, however, when all her friends were praising their husbands, she could not resist bragging, "My husband is the best of all. He can change himself into a snake!" As is well known, gossip travels quickly among women, and the news soon reached the king. He immediately ordered the Brahman brought before him. "You promised that you would never adopt your snake form again but you did. Now you must die for breaking your promise." The Brahman reasoned with him, "My punishment is well-deserved, but the women should also be punished for gossiping." In anger, the king ordered the execution of all the women who had spread the gossip. "Ah, then your own wife must die, too," said the Brahman, and the king sadly realized his mistake. "All right then," the Brahman conceded, "the women shall not be executed, but merely given five strokes of the cane, and the snake shall be worshipped on Nāg Pañcamī."

Even today, dolls representing the women are beaten on Nāg Pañcamī, and snakes are worshipped.[3] (MAHADEVI—70—KANPUR CITY).

NOTES

1. See Gupte 1919: 176.
2. See "Manasa" in Gupte 1919.
3. See "The Story of the Doom of Parikshit" and "The Sacrifice of Janamejaya" in Nivedita 1975: 9; "Gurui Festival—A Snake Legend" in *North Indian Notes and Queries*, 1 (5): 73 (August 1891); Lall 1933: 131; and Dimmit 1978: 286.

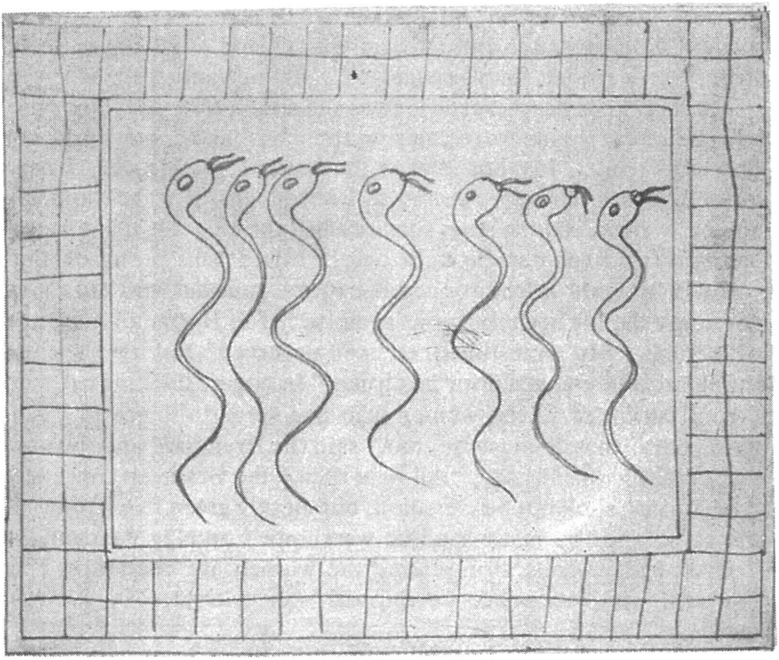

Plate 1. Nāg Pañcamī
A wall painting, made with lampblack, showing seven snakes.
(Rani Misra—34—Delhi).

V. BAHURĀ CAUTH

Bahurā Cauth is observed by women who are blessed with a son or sons, on the fourth day in the dark half of the month of Bhādau. On this day, women sculpt clay images of a lion, a cow, and her calf and place them on a *pāṭā* (flat wooden seat). Parched chickpeas are put in mangers in front of the lion, cow, and calf (see Plate 2). Parched chickpeas, cucumbers, and *nārī* (a kind of green vegetable) are offered in the worship.

After worshipping the images and telling the story given below, women worship a live cow that has a calf. For the rest of the day they eat pūrīs made out of chickpea flour, avoiding all food prepared with wheat, rice, or milk.

9. THE COW AND THE LION

Once there was a cow who lived near a stream with her calves. A lion lived on the other side of the stream. Usually the lion drank the water from his side and the cow drank water from her side, waiting until the lion had drunk first. One day, however, the cow drank water before the lion and her saliva floated downstream to the spot where the lion was drinking. The cow's saliva tasted so sweet that he thought, "The cow's meat must also be very sweet and tender."

The lion went to the cow and said, "I want to eat you!" The cow became nervous at the thought of being eaten, but said to the lion, "First let me go nurse my calves, then I will come to be eaten by you." At first the lion thought the cow was trying to trick him, but the cow promised that she would return, so he let her go.

When the cow came back to her calves, they noticed that their mother was shivering and her milk was very hot. They asked her why she was upset, but she told them, "Drink my milk and grow as gentle as a cow should be." Then the cow tied up her calves, bid them all farewell, and set off to meet her doom. Her calves knew that something was wrong, however, and all of them broke their ropes and followed her.

Meanwhile, the lion was watching from the top of a hill. When he saw the cow coming with all her calves following close behind, he thought, "What a kind-hearted cow! Not only is she keeping her promise to return to be eaten, she is also bringing her calves for me to eat. This food will last me a long time." Before the cow reached the lion, however, her calves ran up and begged him, "Dear maternal uncle, eat us first!" The lion was in a dilemma. He finally decided he could not hurt them, since they had called him "maternal uncle". He promised them, "Now that I am your maternal uncle and you are my nieces and nephews, you may all enjoy the freedom of this forest. No harm will ever come to you." The lion hung a bell on a tree and added. "If you are ever in trouble, ring this bell and I will come to your aid immediately."

Thus the cow and her calves were spared by the lion and gained his protection as well. One day the calves decided to test the bell; they rang it and the lion came running immediately. When he saw that he had been called for no good reason, the lion told the calves, "You should not have done that. Now I will never know whether I should answer the bell or not."

The next morning some hunters came to the forest and began stalking the calves. The calves rang the bell immediately, but the lion was busy eating his prey and thought that the calves were playing practical jokes again, so he didn't go to their aid. The hunters soon captured the calves and took them away.

That evening the lion found the cow weeping and learned that the calves had been taken by the hunters. "There is nothing I can do now, Sister," the lion tried to console her, "but from now on you can live freely in the forest."[1] (PHOOLMATI—81—SHEOLI).

9a. VARIATION ON STORY NO. 9

In this variation, a *kapilā* (domestic cow) goes to the forest with a *harahaiyā* (undomestic cow). A lion tastes her saliva in the stream and decides to eat her, whereupon she tells him that she has one calf and six heifers and must go home to feed the calf before she is eaten. The lion makes the cow vow three times that she will return.

While the cow cares for her calf and heifers, she tells them to be gentle and never go to the forest, and she tells the calf to drink the milk until his belly is full. Her children notice that their mother is sad and nervous and her milk has turned to blood. They ask her what is wrong, but she will not tell them, so they follow her when she leaves. When they see the lion, they run up to him and say, "Dear maternal uncle, eat us before you eat our mother." The lion then blesses them and says, "*Ham māmā tum bhaine, chiṭak carau kajarī ban, piyau sārā tāl*" (Now that you have made me your maternal uncle, you shall all live in peace and happiness). Thus the cow's life was spared.[2] (BETI DEVI—85—SHEOLI).

NOTES

1. See Ayer 1975: 64; Pandey 1967: 74; Roy-Chaudhury 1976: 36; Satyendra 1957: 312; and "The Cow and the Tigress" in *North Indian Notes and Queries*, 3 (7): 122 (October 1893).
2. Similar stories with minor variations were recorded from Bhagwati Shukla—54—Varanasi; K.K. Misra—41—Sheoli; Bhagwati Pandey—57—Kanpur city; and Mahadevi—70—Kanpur city.

Plate 2. Bahurā Cauth
Sculpture made on a wooden board (18" x 9") with clay, depicting a lion, a cow, and her calf, eating parched chickpeas from their mangers. The images are decorated with unhusked wheat. Cucumbers are part of the food offered in worship. (Sheela Pandey—26—Kanpur city).

VI. HARACHAṬH

Harachaṭh is a fast performed by women to assure the well-being of their sons; it is observed on the sixth day of the dark half of Bhādau. Only mothers of sons are required to observe this fast, although women without sons also observe it frequently, in hopes of being blessed with sons. A portion of wall is plastered with cowdung paste upon which a depiction of Mother Harachaṭh is painted with aipan (see Plates 3, 4, and 5).

On this day, women who observe the worship do not partake of cow's milk, oil, or grain grown by ploughing, nor do they cross ploughed fields or lines of black ants. In preparation for the worship, seven kinds of grain and pulses (*canā*, chickpeas; *makāī*, corn; *bājarā*, millet; *gehūṅ*, wheat; *cāval*, rice; *maṭar*, peas; and *jvār*, a kind of millet) are parched and put into *cukaḍiyā*s (small clay pots). These pots are kept in front of the painting of Mother Harachaṭh. Many varieties of food are offered and at least six stories are told. After each story, flowers are showered on the painting and everyone present says, "Victory to Mother Harachaṭh!" Afterwards, twigs of *jālī-chūlī* (also called *jharaberī* and *palās*) are stuck in the ground of the courtyard. The images of a lion, a cow, and her calf, made on the day of Bahurā Cauth, are put under these twigs and worshipped with yogurt, *pasaī ke cāval* (wild rice), and *mahuā* fruit. Then each woman participating eats a little yogurt and wild rice on a palās leaf, six times, to break the fast.

10. THE COWHERD FAMILY AND THE SHE-BUFFALO

Once there was an *ahīr* (cowherd) family which had one old she-buffalo. On the day of Harachaṭh, the mother of the family told her daughter-in-law, "Don't beat the she-buffalo today. Worship her instead." The daughter-in-law promised to treat the she-buffalo with kindness and her mother-in-law went to the fields. The daughter-in-law worked hard cleaning and sweeping the barn, but as soon as she was done, the old she-buffalo made a loose bowel movement on the ground. The daughter-in-law cleaned up the mess, but the animal defecated again. The daughter-in-law cleaned up again, but when she-buffalo defecated a third time, the daughter-in-law lost her temper and hit the she-buffalo with her broom, shouting, "Get out of here!" Driven out of the house, the poor she-buffalo went to the *Kajarī* forest, with her calf following along behind her.

That evening when the mother-in-law came from the fields, she saw that the animals were missing and asked her daughter-in-law where they were. She answered, "I cleaned the whole barn three times, and each time the she-buffalo made a loose bowel movement; finally I hit her and untied her, and she left with her calf."

The mother-in-law was upset and went in search of her she-buffalo. She found her in the *Kajarī* forest and asked her, "Why are you sitting here?" The she-buffalo told her, "Your daughter-in-law rules the house now, so I cannot live there anymore." The mother-in-law begged her, "Stay at my house as long as I live, at least," and persuaded her to return home. Then the mother-in-law performed the worship of Harachaṭh.[1] (BHAGWATI PANDEY—57—KANPUR CITY).

10a. VARIATION ON STORY NO. 10

There once were a mother-in-law and daughter-in-law. One day the daughter-in-law was sweeping the place where the female buffalo was tied. The buffalo was digesting her food, but the daughter-in-law thought she was making faces at her and thus hit the buffalo with her broom. The beast became angry, broke her rope, and went to the jungle. When the mother-in-law came, she asked where the buffalo was. The daughter-in-law said, "I don't know. The buffalo was making faces at me, so I hit her with the broom and then she left." In the meantime, all the milk and yogurt in the house had gotten covered with spider webs. Seeing this, the mother-in-law went out to look for the buffalo. She found her in the forest and asked her to come back home with her. The buffalo replied, "No, your time is over; you no longer run the house. Your daughter-in-law hit me, so I will not come back." Nevertheless, the mother-in-law persuaded the buffalo to return. She washed the buffalo and promised, "You will remain in my house as long as I am alive." (RAMKALI MISRA—62—SHEOLI).

11. THE DAUGHTER-IN-LAW BURNS THE SERVANT'S CHILDREN

Once a milkmaid lived with her daughter-in-law. On the day of Harachaṭh, she told her daughter-in-law, "Fry these mahuā fruits by burning *ṭhiñguriyāñ-muñgariyāñ* (twigs and small branches)." Then the mother-in-law left for the fields, taking her maidservant with her.

By chance, the maidservant happened to have two sons named Thinguriya and Mungariya. The daughter-in-law was so stupid that she thought that her mother-in-law meant for her to burn the boys. She built a fire, used the boys for fuel, and fried the mahuā. When that was done, she cleaned the kitchen and threw the ashes from the fire into the garbage area.

Once the maidservant's work with the mother-in-law was done, she meant to return home, but a row of black ants progressed steadily across her path. The maidservant was a pious woman and would not cross a row of black ants on the day of Harachaṭh, so she waited patiently until evening, when the row of ants broke, and then returned home.

Meanwhile, the milkmaid had returned home. Seeing that the maidservant's sons were missing, she asked her daughter-in-law where they were. "I burned them in the fire, as you told me," answered the stupid girl. "I meant for you to burn twigs and small branches, not the children!" wailed her mother-in-law. "How am I going to tell the maidservant of this misfortune?"

Because of the maidservant's devotion to Mother Harachaṭh, however, her sons came back to life in the heap of ashes and thus their mother found them playing in the garbage when she came home. She picked both of them up and went to the milkmaid, complaining, "Because I am poor, my children are left unattended to play in the garbage." The incredulous mother-in-law threw herself at her servant's feet and told her, "Your sons were dead, burned alive by my daughter-in-law! May Mother Harachaṭh bless everyone as she has blessed you!"[2] (BHAGWATI PANDEY—57—KANPUR CITY).

12. A MOTHER'S LOVE

Once there was a mother whose son lived away from home with his wife. On the day of Harachaṭh, the mother gathered all the materials for the worship: many kinds of parched grains, small earthen pots to hold them and so on. When she had finished, the mother thought, "I want to go and lick my son's body" (an expression of love). The mother disguised herself as a dog and went to her son's house.

When the mother arrived at her son's house, her daughter-in-law was making aipan to color the earthen pots and make the painting for the worship of Harachaṭh, and a barber was applying ubṭan to her son's body. In her disguise as a dog, the mother came up and started licking the dirty ubṭan from her son's body. Seeing this, the daughter-in-law hit the dog with her pestle, leaving a mark on the dog's body. The dog then kept her distance but hung around a while longer to watch and listen. Her son took a bath and then told his wife, "I am going to visit my mother today, because it is Harachaṭh." His wife demanded, "If you go to your mother's house, you must bring me señdur and the parched grains used in the worship of Mother Harachaṭh." Her husband promised to bring these things for her and left for his mother's home.

The mother reached home just before her son did; they spent a pleasant evening together. The next morning when her son was ready to leave, the mother told him, "Take the things which your wife asked you to bring her." The son protested, "She didn't ask me to bring anything." His mother insisted, however, and gave him each item her daughter-in-law had asked for. "How did you know exactly what she wanted?" her son questioned. "When you were having your ubṭan bath, I came as a dog so that I could lick your body. This is the mark where your wife hit me," answered his mother.

The son was so touched by his mother's love and affection that he came back to live with her from that day onward.[3] (BHAGWATI PANDEY—57—KANPUR CITY).

13. THE FOOLISH DAUGHTER-IN-LAW FEEDS THE BROOM

Once there lived a mother-in-law and a daughter-in-law. One day when the mother-in-law was leaving to visit her parents' home, she asked her daughter-in-law to take good care of the broom (*i.e.*, to keep the household tidy). The daughter-in-law was a little thick-headed and didn't really understand what her mother-in-law meant. Each morning and evening she put two roṭīs over the broom. She didn't handle the broom well, in any case, and whenever she swept, several twigs came out. By the time her mother-in-law returned, the house was a mess and the broom was ruined. "I told you to take good care of the broom," she scolded her daughter-in-law. "But I did," insisted the girl. "I gave it two roṭīs every morning and evening."

This upset the mother-in-law, who thought, "My daughter-in-law is crazy." She therefore told her son to take his wife back to her home. To please his mother, the son took his wife out of the house. He could not bear to banish her completely, however, so he hid her in a pile of cowdung cakes. He stole roṭīs and other food at every meal and slipped them to his wife when no one was looking. Time passed and eventually she was blessed with a son. Her husband took care of everythig without his mother's knowledge.

On the day of Harachaṭh, it seemed that every other household was worshipping, singing, and making merry. The mother-in-law thought sadly to herself, "I wish that my crazy daughter-in-law was here, so that we could have singing and merrymaking in my house also. I might have also had a grandson to enjoy." When the son discovered his mother in a state of depression, he asked, "Why are you so sad today?" She regretted, "If I hadn't banished your wife, I might have been blessed with a grandson and could have celebrated the worship of Mother Harachaṭh today." Her son laughed and teased her. "Will you keep your daughter-in-law if I can find her?" "Oh, yes, yes," she agreed joyfully. "Do you know where she is?" He led her to the place where the cowdung cakes were kept. She was overjoyed to see her daughter-in-law with a baby boy sucking on her breasts. The daughter-in-law immediately laid her son on her mother-in-law's feet and prostrated herself before her. With great joy, the mother-in-law brought her back to her house and worshipped Mother Harachaṭh.[4] (PHOOLMATI—81—SHEOLI).

14. A SON SACRIFICED TO THE POND

Once a woman lived alone with her son. Her brother had dug a pond, but water would not stay in it. When a priest told him, "Sacrifice a child to the pond and it will become full of water," the brother thought of his sister's son. He went to persuade her, "Send your son to live with me, so that he can be educated and enjoy a more comfortable life." His sister agreed happily, so he carried the boy off. Then he sacrified his nephew to the pond, which immediately filled with water and beautiful flowers.

On the day of Harachaṭh, the sister thought, "I have only one son, so I will go to my brother's house and see my son and perform the worship of Harachaṭh there." As she passed the beautiful pond, she noticed her son lying on a big leaf in the middle. She was unable to reach the child and came running up to her brother, scolding, "You have not been taking good care of my son. Look, he is lying on a leaf in the middle of your pond." Upon hearing this, the brother begged his sister's forgiveness and told her, "I sacrified your son to the pond, but Mother Harachaṭh has given him back to you."[5] (PUSHPALATA—41—SHEOLI).

14a. VARIATION ON STORY NO. 14

In this variation, the characters are king and queen, instead of brother and sister. The king decides to kill their only son when his priest tells him, "Sacrifice a child on the day of Harachaṭh and your empty tank will have water." To get rid of the queen, the king insists that she visit her ailing mother. When the queen finds that her mother is all right, she suspects some treachery and returns home immediately. She tells the palanquin carriers to pass the new tank on the way home, so that she can see why there is no water in it. She finds the tank full of water and her son, who had been sacrified by the king, playing in the water. The king is afraid to open the door when the queen arrives, but she tells him, "I am not angry. I found our son alive, because of my devotion to Mother Harachaṭh. Open the door and let us in." Then they all lived happily together. (PUSHPALATA—41—SHEOLI).

15. WHY COW AND BUFFALO MILK SHOULD NOT BE MIXED

Once there was an ahīr family which had many cows and buffalos and lived a comfortable life by selling their milk. Their customers asked them not to mix the milk of cows and buffalos together on the day of Harachaṭh, since only buffalo milk is consumed on that day. The daughter-in-law of the ahīr family ignored this request and proceeded to mix the milk and distribute it. As soon as she did this, all of her family's animals died. When she returned, her mother-in-law asked her, "Did you do something wrong?" At first the daughter-in-law denied doing anything, but when she learned that all the animals had died, she confessed to mixing the cow and buffalo milk together.

The mother-in-law then went to everyone who had received milk that day and told them, "My daughter-in-law mistakenly mixed the cow and buffalo milk today. Please don't use it in your worship." After thus informing each customer, the mother-in-law returned home and found all her animals alive and well again.[6] (BHAGWATI PANDEY—57—KANPUR CITY).

16. I CAN'T CROSS PLOUGHED FIELDS TODAY

On the day of Harachaṭh, a man set off to plough his field. His mother tried to dissuade him, but he said, "Harachaṭh is for women. There is no reason why I cannot plough today." While ploughing, he was bitten by a snake and fell dead in the middle of the field.

His mother was busy worshipping Harachaṭh, when someone ran up to inform her, "Your son is lying dead in the middle of the field." As soon as she heard this, the mother ran to the field. Since the field was ploughed, she could not cross it; she ran frantically around the boundaries, sobbing:

Hāy āj jotā khāvaṅ,	Alas, today I shouldn't eat any ploughed food,
na jotā rauṅdoṅ;	nor should I cross ploughed fields;
Hāy āj lalā ke mare,	Alas, because of my son's death today,
Haradaudoṅ hoigai.	I have worshipped Harachaṭh in vain.

Mother Harachaṭh saw all this and thought, "This woman is observing my worship so faithfully that she will not cross a ploughed field even to reach her dead son." The goddess therefore brought the woman's son back to life. He sat up and saw his mother running around the field weeping. "Why are you crying, Mother?" he asked in bewilderment. "Because of you, dear son." He came to her and she told him what had happened. They walked home together in joy and thankfulness. (PHOOLMATI—81—SHEOLI).

16a. VARIATION ON STORY NO. 16

On the day of Harachaṭh, an ahīr man went to plough his field, telling his wife, "Bring my lunch as usual." She protested, "Please wait and take your lunch with you, for today is Harachaṭh and I cannot cross a ploughed field." "I don't believe in any of that," grumbled the ahīr, "and I am taking our son along with me. You will surely come to bring food for him, despite your silly beliefs." The woman brought food to the edge of the field and was horrified to witness the death of her son on the sharp point of the plough. She still refused to cross the field, saying, "*Jotā khāy na jotā rauṅde, āj hāi Haradaudoṅ*" (One should not eat cultivated food or cross cultivated fields, today is Harachaṭh). Thus the woman sat on the edge of the field, crying the whole day and on into the night.

Mother Harachaṭh came to her, disguised as an old woman, and asked her, "Why are you sitting here crying?" The mother sobbed, "I long to touch the body of my dead son, but today is Harachaṭh and I cannot cross the ploughed field where he is lying. I must wait until tomorrow to pick him up and take him home to perform the death rituals." Touched by the mother's devotion, Mother Harachaṭh went into the field, lifted up the son, and gave him back to his mother alive. Thus the woman won her son back because of her strong beliefs. (BHAGWATI PANDEY—57—KANPUR CITY).

17. WATCH MY SON WHILE I SELL MILK

On the day of Harachaṭh, a milkmaid set off to sell her buffalo milk. On the way, she met a farmer who was ploughing his fields. "Will you watch my baby while I go sell my milk?" she requested. The farmer promised to look after the baby, but later forgot about it and accidentally ran the plough over it. The frightened farmer hid the baby's body underneath a jālī-chūlī bush and went home.

After a while the milkmaid returned, but she couldn't find either her child or the farmer. She searched around and eventually saw her child lying under the jālī-chūlī bush, babbling happily. She picked up the child and went to the farmer's home to complain, "You should not have left my child alone." The farmer confessed what had happened and told her in admiration, "Because of your devotion on the day of Harachaṭh, your child has come back to life." (BETI DEVI—85—SHEOLI).

18. REWARD AND PUNISHMENT UNDER THE *CHIKULIYĀ* TREE

There once lived a Jeṭhānī and a Devarānī. On the day of the festival of Harachaṭh, Devarānī was keeping fast. (During the fast, the fasting person eats ñarī and wild rice, *khoyā* [milk which has been thickened by boiling], or fruits.) At Jeṭhānī's parents' house, many food preparations were usually made, because they had a good supply of rice and a milk-giving buffalo. Devarānī therefore decided to go to Jeṭhānī's house, so that she could eat her fill of rice with yogurt. On her way through the forest, Devarānī plucked leaves from the chikuliyā trees, saying: "Chikuliyā, give me your leaves, so that I can use them as a plate for the rice I will eat at Jeṭhānī's parents' house." When Devarānī arrived at Jeṭhānī's parents' house, Jeṭhānī whispered to her mother, "If you give her rice to eat, she will tell my in-laws that we eat only rice here, nothing else." As a result, Jeṭhānī's mother didn't offer any rice to Devarānī. Disappointed, Devarānī set off for home and returned the leaves to the chikuliyā trees, saying: "Take your leaves, chikuliyā, I didn't get any rice at my Jeṭhānī's house." She was keeping fast, but had not done the worship. Tired, she laid under a chikuliyā tree and fell asleep. Mother Harachaṭh observed this and thought, "This woman is most sincere in my worship." As a reward, Mother Harachaṭh put a sack full of rice and a bowl of yogurt under the chikuliyā tree for her. When Devarānī awoke, she found those items and brought them home. There she prepared the meal and ate it. In the meantime, Jeṭhānī returned and asked, "What have you eaten, since you didn't get anyting at my house?" Devarānī replied, "Mother Harachaṭh gave me rice and yogurt to eat." Jeṭhānī asked her how this came about, so Devarānī told her exactly what had happened.

The next year Jeṭhānī went to Devarānī's parents' house. Devarānī told her mother to feed her as much rice as she could eat. Jeṭhānī ate her fill; on her way back home, she lay down under a tree. Mother Harachaṭh thought, "She is pretending to be sincere," so she left a sack full of sand and a bowl of mud for her. When Jeṭhānī brought them home and found the sand and mud, she began arguing and fighting with Devarānī, "You lied to me!" Then Devarānī replied, "Dear Jeṭhānī, you were pretending, but I was truly poor." (MAHADEVI—70—KANPUR CITY).

NOTES

1. A similar story was also recorded from Beti Devi—85—Sheoli.
2. See "Baj Baras" in Parmar 1969:331 and Sita 1970:84. Similar stories were recorded from Beti Devi—85—Sheoli; Phoolmati—81—Sheoli; Sukhrani Devi—70—Sheoli; and Mahadevi—70—Kanpur city.
3. A similar story was also recorded from Mahadevi—70—Kanpur city.
4. The same informant told the same story the previous year for the worship of Bahurā Cauth.
5. See Sita 1970:72. A similar story was also recorded from Mahadevi—70—Kanpur city.
6. A similar story was recorded from Phoolmati—81—Sheoli. In her version, she specifies that the daughter-in-law mixes the cow and buffalo milk out of greed. The mother-in-law makes the daughter-in-law go to each customer herself.

Plate 3. Harachath

A wall painting made with rice paste, showing four cows and three calves, a tulsī plant, svastiks, a stone slab and muller, Ganga-Yamuna, small clay pots, a bucket, a married couple, an elephant, a toy, the sun and moon, a *kajarauṭī*, flowers, and the altar of Mother Harachath. Concentric circles are drawn in front of the altar and some of the clay pots filled with parched grains are placed there during the worship. (Rani Misra—34—Delhi).

Plate 4. Harachath

A wall painting made with rice paste, depicting Mother Harachath as a supreme deity with four arms. Inside the square which forms her body are clay pots, cows, a tulsī plant, children, Ganga-Yamuna, a comb, a *kajarauṭī*, the sun and moon, a potter woman carrying clay pots, a stone slab and muller, toys, and svastiks. (Rani Misra—34—Delhi).

Plate 5. Harachath

A wall painting, made with rice paste, showing a cow and an ox, a tulsī plant, turtles, Shiv and Parvati, a flower, a svastik, the sun and moon, Gods Ganesh and Hanuman, and Ganga-Yamuna. In the middle of the painting Mother Harachath protects numerous children (Choti Bitiya—27—Sheoli).

VII. AVAĪ ĀTHAĪ

Avaī Āṭhaī is a fast observed by married women, on the eighth day of the dark half of Kārtik, to ensure motherhood and to protect children already born. Women fast the whole day, and pictures of the Goddess Avaī Āṭhaī (see Plate 6) and a *Turkin* (A Turkish woman), in some homes, are painted on the walls. In the evening the paintings and the moon are worshipped with pharā and *phulaurī*. The festival is also known as *Turkin Pūjā* (see Story No. 22).

Pandey (1967:148) examines the Muslim influence on this worship and points out that this fast is called *Ashok Asṭamī* in the *Purans* and has been popular among Hindus for generations. Hindus who converted to Islam probably continued the observance of this fast. Turkin means wife of a Turk (*i.e.*, a Muslim woman); the implications of naming this ritual Turkin Puja are obvious.

19. AHOI'S DEVOTION TO HER CHILDREN

There once lived a woman named Ahoi who had eight children.[1] Although she was poor, she loved her children dearly and somehow managed to take care of all of them. Yam wanted to take some of her children and give them to childless women. Therefore he told one *Yamdūt* (the messenger of Yam) to go to Ahoi's house. "When you hear her say, '*maraiñ mari jāv khaṭiyā kāḍhe marat nāhīñ haiñ*' (Die, you troublemakers), bring one of the children to me."

So Yamdūt went to Ahoi's house, hiding himself so he could hear what went on there. One day she cooked some food for her children, but they were fighting among themselves and complained, "There is not enough space for us all to sit down." Ahoi pacified them, saying, "Dear children, there are only eight of you, but there is so much space that I could have eight more children and still you all would have room to sit."

Yamdūt related this incident to Yam, but Yam said, "Keep watching," Yamdūt returned, and before long another fight arose over the drinking water. Several of the children cried, "I didn't get enough to drink." Ahoi soothed them again, saying, "Even if I had four more children, you all could satisfy your thirst from this cup." Again Yamdūt reported to Yam, but Yam told him to watch what happened that night. Yamdūt returned to Ahoi's house and observed that there was not much bedding for the children. One child was complaining, "I'm cold!" while another child wept, "I don't have enough to cover me." Ahoi put her big skirt around the children, saying, "Come here, darlings. There is so much space that I could cover four more children besides you. Go to sleep now." Yamdūt made his third report to Yam, and Yam decided to let all of Ahoi's children stay with her, since she was so devoted to them.[2] (PHOOLMATI—81—SHEOLI).

20. DON'T DIG MUD TODAY

Once a Nanad lived with a peace-loving *Bhaujāī* (elder brother's wife). Both of them fasted on the day of Avaī Āṭhaī, but Nanad started digging some mud. "Don't dig mud today," pleaded bhaujāī, "for you will kill many insects in doing so." However, Nanad did not heed her words.

Time passed, and eventually both of them died. Bhaujāī was reborn as a *murgī* (hen), and Nanad as a *kuṭkuṭī* (a bird). Murgī was blessed with seven chicks, but all the kuṭkuṭī's babies died. Kuṭkuṭī was so jealous that she tried to kill murgī's chicks, but Mother Avai Āṭhaī protected them. Finally kuṭkuṭī went to murgī and asked her, "What worship and fasting do you observe that all of your babies are alive and none of mine have survived?" Murgī answered, "In our former lives, you were my nanad and I was your bhaujāī. On the day of the Avaī Āṭhaī worship, you insisted on digging mud and thus killed many insects. That is why your babies do not survive. However, if you worship Mother Avaī Āṭhaī now, you will be blessed with babies." Kuṭkuṭī took murgī's advice, performed the worship, and soon hatched a baby that survived.[3] (SUKHRANI DEVI—70—SHEOLI).

21. PROPITIATING MOTHER PORCUPINE

Once there lived a Nanad and a Bhaujāī. When they visited farms, Nanad used to break *syāhī* (porcupine) eggs. Bhaujāī tried to stop her, but Nanad said, "I feel awful when I see those eggs, so I must kill them."

Time passed and Nanad was married. Her children never survived, however, and her husband and in-laws got so worried that they consulted a priest. He told them, "Your daughter-in-law killed many syāhī eggs when she was young; Mother Syāhī is angry with her and thus carries her children away. There is one remedy, however. Wash your house and celebrate a festival in honor of Mother Syāhī. When Mother Syāhī comes for the celebration, your daughter-in-law should prostrate in front of her. Then Mother Syāhī will bless her with a long life and many children. After the feast, your daughter-in-law should pick the fleas from Mother Syāhī's hair, then put her child on her lap and pinch him to make him cry. Mother Syāhī will say, "Don't bother to look for my fleas; take care of your child." Your daughter-in-law should tell her, "He is not crying because he needs my care; he wants your earrings."

The worship of Mother Syāhī was promptly arranged and Nanad did everything according to the priest's instructions. When she asked for earrings for the child, Mother Syāhī answered, "You have asked too much, but I will give them to you." As soon as Mother Syāhī gave her earrings to Nanad, her children began to survive.[4] (PHOOLMATI—81—SHEOLI)

22. TURKIN OFFERS FOOD TO THE MOON

Once there was a woman whose children never survived. When she got pregnant again, she worried greatly and asked an older woman what she should do. The woman advised her, "On the night of Avaī Āṭhaī, use the end of your sari to collect the *pharā* and *phulaurī* which the Turkin offers to the moon at midnight. If you eat these, you will be blessed with a child who lives."

As soon as the moon came out on the night of Avaī Āṭhaī, the pregnant woman left her house. "Where are you going?" questioned her mother-in-law. "To urinate," she replied, slipping quickly away. In the light of the moon, she saw the Turkin preparing for the worship; as soon as the Turkin threw the pharā and phulaurī towards the moon, the woman caught them in her sari, ate them, and went home. Soon her labor pains began, and shortly thereafter a son was born, with pharā and phulaurī in his mouth. The women who assisted in the birth wanted to remove the pharā and phulaurī from the newborn's mouth, but the mother cried out, "No! Leave them alone." And thus her son survived.

For this reason, a painting of the Turkin is made on the day of Avaī Āṭhaī, and women worship it.[5] (BETI DEVI—85—SHEOLI).

NOTES

1. This informant had told the same story the previous year with the following differences: the woman was not named and had sixteen children.
2. In a similar story, told by Sukhrani Devi—70—Sheoli, the woman has seven children and worships Avaī Āṭhaī faithfully. In preparation for the worship, the woman goes to the well to fetch fresh water. There *Jam-Jaminā* (Yam and his wife) see her and decide to take one of her children. However, during the worship, they hear the woman pray, "Oh, Mother Avaī Āṭhaī, bless me with another child." Realizing how devoted she is to her children, Jam-Jaminā decide to leave them in peace.
3. The same informant told this same story a year later, but did not mention rebirth in other forms. Nanad's children do not survive and she asks her why. She tells her, "You killed many insects while you were digging mud, neglecting my advice. That's why your children don't survive. Next year, when women are worshipping the moon at midnight on the day of Avaī Āṭhaī, collect their offerings in the end of your sari. Eat them, and you will be blessed with a son." See also Lewis 1965:218
4. See Pandey 1967:153. Even today, if a woman's children do not survive, her sister's earrings are used to make a needle for piercing the next child's ear and nose. Women believe that this will help the child survive, because earrings from a mother's sister's ear are considered auspicious.
5. See Pandey 1967:152; it is also of interest to note that "Turkin" was the special title for goddess Sītalā around the turn of the century near Hardwar (Crooke 1896:1.126).

Plate 6. Avaī Āṭhaī

A wall painting, made with rice paste, showing seven children with karva pots, the potter and his wife selling karvas, Ganga-Yamuna, the sun and moon, a peacock and other birds, Gods Ganesh and Hanuman, svastiks, a fan, a *kajarauṭī*, and a toy. Mother Āvaī Aṭhaī is placed prominently in the center of the painting. (Rani Misra—34— Delhi).

VIII. CIRAIYĀ GAUR

Ciraiyā Gaur is celebrated on the first day of the bright half of Kārtik.

It is observed by the married women to assure their husband's love for the coming year. Each woman puts some rice into an earthen pot on the night of *Dīpāvalī*, covers it with an earthen saucer, and keeps a lamp burning over it the whole night. The next morning she grinds the rice into flour, kneads it into dough, molds the image of a bird, and cooks it. The women of the household then worship their birds (Ciraiyā Gaur) with señdur and different types of lentils, tell stories, and eat their rice birds in silence.

The festival of Annakūṭ[2] also falls on this day. Only after performing the ritual of Ciraiyā Gaur described above, do women begin preparations for Annakūṭ.

Following stories are told during the worship.

23. A CHARM TO WIN A HUSBAND'S LOVE

Once there was a man who didn't love his wife at all and beat her regularly. The poor woman finally confided her sorrow to another woman, who told her to try this remedy: "Soak some rice on the night of Dīpāvalī. Early the next morning, before sunrise and before any birds warble, grind the rice and make the image of a sparrow from it. Pray to Ciraiyā Gaur and eat the bird from the tail to the head. During the whole time, from the grinding to the eating, you must make no sound with your mouth. If you do all this faithfully, your husband will start loving you."

The unloved woman did as she was told, but she forgot how she was supposed to eat the sparrow, and started from the head, instead of the tail. Days and weeks passed, but her husband didn't change at all. Finally, the woman went to her friend again and told her exactly how she had performed the ritual. Her friend corrected her, "You should have eaten it from the tail. That's why your husband hasn't started loving you."

The next year the woman followed the correct procedure. From that moment on, her husband became loving towards her. (BHAGWATI SHUKLA—54—VARANASI).

23a. VARIATION ON STORY NO. 23

There was a woman who performed the worship of Ciraiyā Gaur, but complained that her husband still beat her. Her friend said, "Maybe you are not worshipping in the correct manner. What do you do?" The woman explained that she soaked some rice, ground it into flour, and made a bird, which she worshipped from the head and ate from the head. "Aha," said her friend, "you must worship it from the head and eat it from the tail. Then your husband will love you." The next year, the woman performed the worship in the manner that her friend prescribed, but still her husband did not act lovingly toward her. She went to her friend again, who said, "You must live nicely and dress nicely."

The woman collected some *caurāī* greens and boiled them. Then she bathed in that boiled water, with the result that her whole body became covered with blisters. Many of the blisters broke open and flies swarmed around her body. When the woman's husband passed by, many of the flies flew away and she said, "*Cauraiyā ne asar janāyā, au piyā māchī hakat āye*" (the caurāī greens are effective, my husband is fanning the flies away). Her husband asked his mother, "What is my wife saying?" His mother replied, "You don't ever speak kindly to your wife. She thinks that the caurāī is a love-potion which made you take care of her by brushing the flies away from her sores." After this incident, the husband started to love his wife.[3] (PHOOLMATI—81—SHEOLI).

24. THE HELL OF INSECTS

On the day of Ciraiyā Gaur, in one household, the grandmother had spread rice after washing the grains. Her granddaughter was very dear to her, but she ate some of the rice and thus made it unfit for the worship. The child's mother came and said, "This rice is now spoiled." The grandmother insisted, "Such doings by children are excusable; you can make your bird from this rice." The mother warned, "The punishment for making a bird from this rice will go to you." The grandmother said, "I don't care; just don't beat my granddaughter." The mother made the bird from the rice that child had nibbled on, and worshipped according to custom.

When the grandmother died, she was thrown into the Hell of Insects by the God of Death. As it happened, the granddaughter was reborn in the God of Death's house. When the granddaughter became a young woman, she remembered and recognized her grandmother in the Hell of Insects. She pretended to be unconscious, so the God of Death came and asked, "What is wrong?" "I have a headache," replied the girl. "How can it be cured?" asked the God of Death. His daughter answered, "My headache will be cured only if you take this old woman out of the insect pit." The God of Death replied, "She committed a sin by telling her daughter-in-law to mold a bird from defiled rice; that's why she cannot be liberated." His daughter persisted, "How can she gain her liberation now?" The God of Death answered, "If a kilo of mustard seeds is thrown into a lumpy field of clods and this old woman picks up every seed, she will be liberated." Thus the old grandmother began picking up mustard seeds every day. She soon got frustrated, however, and said, "I can't pick up all those seeds; I'd rather be in the insect pit." She was thrown back into the insect pit, where her granddaughter found her again. Guiltily, she thought, "It was I who defiled the rice, yet my sin has fallen upon my grandmother."

Again she begged her father, the God of Death, to take her grandmother out of the insect pit. He said, "Since you are pleading so much, there is another chance for your grandmother. She must sell yogurt and persuade a king to donate a bird made of gold; only then can she be liberated." Thus the grandmother began selling milk. It came to pass that she reached a kingdom where the queen was suffering from labor pains, but all the doctors' efforts to help her were in vain. The whole kingdom was gathered in front of the palace, when the grandmother came selling her yogurt. People told her, "Go away! Nobody will buy your yogurt while the queen is suffering in childbirth." The grandmother answered, "I know a remedy which will bring on the birth." She was taken to the king. The grandmother told him, "If you donate a gold bird to charity, your queen will give birth immediately." The king said he was willing to follow her advice, but his queen, knowing what it was all about, said, "No matter what happens, even if I die, do not donate the golden bird." The king ignored the queen's warning and gave a gold bird to charity. Thus the grandmother was liberated and the queen had to suffer the Hell of Insects in her place. (MAHADEVI—70—KANPUR CITY).

25. A SISTER NEGLECTS HER BROTHER'S BIRDS

A girl once lived with her brother, who was very fond of keeping birds. When the time came for the brother's wedding, he asked his sister to care for his birds while he was gone. After the marriage party left for the bride's house, however, the sister got involved in cleaning up and taking care of the guests and forgot to feed the birds. When she finally remembered them, she was horrified to find them all dead in their cages.

The poor girl was very upset, knowing that her brother would be furious when he returned. In desperation, she prayed, "If my brother's birds come back to life, I will host a dinner for the goddess Annakūṭ."

She went outside and stood by the door with 1¼ *paisā* (pice) in her hand. Soon a wedding party passed by; the girl asked the groom, "Please go and buy some chickpeas and raw sugar for me, so that I can worship the goddess Annakūṭ as I have promised." The groom refused, saying, "I am in a hurry," but as soon as he reached his bride's house, he died. After a while some mourners, carrying a dead body, passed the sister's house. She also asked them, "Please go and buy some chickpeas and raw sugar for me, so that I can worship the goddess Annakūṭ as I have promised." One of the dead man's relatives replied, "We are full of sadness and this will delay us for a while, so I will bring what you need for your worship." When the mourner returned with ingredients, the sister performed the worship and distributed prasād. As soon as she finished doing this, the dead man came back to life. The mourners all rejoiced and went home, telling everyone on the way of the miracle that had occurred.

The dead groom's marriage party soon heard of this incident and came back to the sister's house. "What have you done to us?" they wept. "I have done nothing," the sister replied. "The Goddess Annakūṭ has brought this misery upon you, because you proudly refused to bring me the things I needed to worship her."

Upon hearing this, the groom's father prayed to the goddess, I will give a *durakaiyāñ* of 1¼ rupees if my son comes back to life." Then his son also came back to life, the marriage was performed with great happiness, and the groom's father gave the promised durakaiyāñ as soon as they returned home.[4] (PHOOLMATI—81—SHEOLI).

NOTES

1. "When they eat 'rice bird' (chiriyā gaur) lighted with a flame to obtain the unflinching love of their husbands, they are most serious while literally swallowing a flame without quenching it, for to do so would be so inauspicious. They do not practice beforehand for this observance and hence they often burn their palates, but after all the bird is a personification of the goddess Gauri the repository of marital happiness in Hindu thought" (Khare 1976:150).
2. The festival of Annakūṭ is observed in honor of Goddess Annakūṭ, goddess of plenty; fifty-six varieties of food items are cooked. This food is offered to the goddess and then consumed by the family. The plentiful food preparations are said to bring prosperity for the coming year.
3. See Pandey 1967:184.
4. A similar story was told for *Saṅkaṭhā kī Sohāgileñ* by Shivdulari—68—Sheoli.

IX. GOBARDHAN

The Gobardhan worship also falls on first day of the bright half of Kārtik. Men bathe and decorate their animals, especially their prized bullocks. They apply oil to the animals' horns, paint their hooves, and put beads, bells, or colorful cloth on their bodies. Inside the house, women draw a square on the floor with cowdung. Models of houses and temples and figurines of people and animals are molded out of cowdung and placed inside the square, to represent the fortified city of Gokul, which is worshipped with food. In the evening, all the cowdung used in making the city is reshaped into a mountain with face and feet. The stomach is pushed inward and a burning lamp is placed on it. A few wickers are stuck on top of the mountain, to resemble a forest (see Plates 7 and 8). This representation of Mount Gobardhan is placed near the main door of the house, where food is offered to it.[1]

26. THE WORSHIP OF MOUNT GOBARDHAN

In olden times, people performed the worship of the god Indra at Mount Gobardhan. Indra would send down rain only after he was worshipped. One day Krishna transformed himself into the mountain and told the inhabitants of Braj that they could perform Indra's worship right there. When the people brought the food for the offering, however, Krishna ate all of it.

Indra was so angry at Krishna for intercepting his offerings that he unleashed a terrible rainstorm. Rain poured down for eight days; all of Braj was flooded. People were terrified, but Krishna said, "Take shelter under Mount Gobardhan," and lifted the mountain like an umbrella over their heads. The people supported the mountain with their sticks as well, thinking that they were helping to keep it up. After eight days, they got tired and said that they were going to leave. Everyone removed his stick, but the mountain remained aloft, held up by Krishna's little finger. Indra's stock of rainwater soon ran dry and he realized that Krishna was really Vishnu himself. He acknowledged his defeat and stopped the rain.

Since that day, people have worshipped Mount Gobardhan instead of Indra.[2] (BHAGWATI PANDEY—57—KANPUR CITY).

NOTES

1. For descriptions of Gobardhan Puja in other areas, see Chauhan 1967:295; Parmar 1975; Marriott 1955:200; Mathur 1964:109; and Pandey 1967:173.
2. See Marriott 1955:199; "The Lifting of the Mountain" in Nivedita 1975:173; Pandey 1967:173; and Dimmitt 1978:116.

Plate 7. Gobardhan
A drawing made with cowdung, to represent the city of "Gokul, its households and their animals." In the center are Krishna and Balaram. (Chāya Tiwari—22—Kanpur city).

Plate 8. Gobardhan
A sculpture of Mount Gobardhan, made with cowdung, which is worshipped with food offerings. The image is kept near the main door of the house, with an oil lamp burning in the sunken stomach area. The cotton and wickers represent trees in the forest. (Chaya Tiwari—22—Kanpur city).

X. BHAIYĀ DŪJ

Bhaiyā Dūj is observed on the second day of the bright half of Kārtik. Girls and women with brothers make a painting on the floor (see Plate 9), worship the painting, tell stories, apply tilak on their brothers' foreheads, and offer them sweets to eat. Brothers and sisters both keep fast until the tilak is applied.

27. A SISTER'S EXTRAORDINARY DEVOTION

There once lived a boy whose sister was married to a man in a distant land (across the Jamuna and Ganga rivers). On the day of Bhaiyā Dūj, every other man and boy in the village proudly wore a *rocanā* applied by his sister, but this boy's forehead was bare. He felt so sad that he asked his mother for permission to visit his sister. His mother tried to tell him that it was much too far, but he insisted he could make it and set off on his journey.

When the boy arrived at his sister's gate, his sister was making an *araval* (*ayurbal*, continuation of life, has become by a village etymology *araval*) out of cotton for the worship of Bhaiyā Dūj; she took care to finish it before welcoming her brother. The boy thought, "I have come a long way, but my sister is so proud that she won't even get up to greet me." He started to leave, but his sister finished the araval and ran after him, explaining, "I am preparing for Bhaiyā Dūj only because of you; you have no reason to be angry."

The sister was bit simpleminded, so she ran to her neighbor to ask, "What shall I prepare for my brother who has just come? He is my one and only brother and is very dear to me." In jest, the neighbor woman told her, "Smear the kitchen with castor oil, fry pūrīs in milk, and boil rice in ghī to make *khīr*." The sister hastened home and followed her neighbor's instructions to the letter, but her brother disliked the food thus prepared. In distress, she ran to her neighbor's home again, wailing, "I did exactly as you told me, but my brother isn't eating the food I made. What shall I do?" When the neighbor realized how simpleminded the girl really was, she told her seriously, "Smear the kitchen with cowdung, fry pūrīs in ghī, and boil rice in milk to make khīr." Then the sister made the food properly, and the brother enjoyed eating it.

The brother stayed at his sister's house for some time, but one day he told her, "I should return home as our mother will be worried about me." The sister persuaded him to stay just one more night, so that he could get an early start. In the wee hours of the morning, she got up to prepare some food for her brother's journey. It was so dark that she didn't see a snake's skin in the flour and thus mixed it into the pūrī dough. After her brother left, carrying these pūrīs with him, her sons got up and asked for some of the pūrīs made for their maternal uncle. When they saw the snake's skin in the bread, they ran to tell her. She got very upset, thinking, "My brother may have died because of eating the pūrīs I made for him!" She ran down the road to look for him.

Eventually the sister found her brother lying under a tree. She was sure that he was dead, but in her agitation, she began to shake him. Startled out of a sound sleep, he mumbled, "What is the matter?" "Have you eaten any of the pūrīs I gave you?" she asked frantically. "No, they are hanging up on this tree," he answered; she gave a great sigh of relief. "Let me go the rest of the way home with you," she pleaded. "No, you should come with me only when I come to get you," he reasoned, but she insisted on going along.

Thus brother and sister started off for their parents' home together. On the way the sister got thirsty. Her brother pointed, "Look, there are some farmers working over there. They will have a pot and a rope which you can borrow. Go and drink some water from that nearby well." The sister borrowed the pot and rope, but while she was at the well, she overheard them saying, "Yam wants some shoes made out of the heart of a man whose sister has never abused him. A brick will fall on him or a snake will bite him during his wedding." She thought to herself, "I have never abused my brother, so maybe he is the man Yam is looking for." She ran from the well, abusing her brother badly, saying, "*Bhaiyā marai bhaujaiyā rāṅḍ hoy*" (May my brother die and my brother's wife become a widow), thus making many holes in his heart.

Eventually the brother and sister reached their parents' home. When their mother and father heard the girl abusing her brother so badly, they thought she had gone mad and locked her in a room. The brother's marriage was arranged, but the sister insisted on going along and having each ceremony performed on herself before it was performed on her brother. When the brick fell, she picked it up; when the snake came, she put it in her bag. The marriage thus proceeded without any difficulty. When the bride and groom returned to the groom's home, the sister insisted on sleeping between the couple. She had learned from the farmers that her brother's death would occur during his wedding, but she was determined to prevent it.

Because of her intervention, Yam's servants had failed to take her brother's life, so they returned to Yam. He instructed them, "Go to the room where the bride and groom are supposed to spend their *suhāgrāt* (nuptial night) together. When you see two heads, four legs, and four feet, take the life of the man." Yam's servants went to the room, as they were told, but they found three heads, six legs, and six feet. They reported this to Yam, who was forced to acknowledge his defeat, because of the sister's love for her brother.

After the wedding, all the guests were given appropriate gifts at the time of their departure. The girl's parents thought that this would be a good time to get rid of her also, so they selected some clothes to give to her. All of these clothes turned into beautiful saris, however, which perplexed her parents. Then their daughter came out of her room and told them, "I don't want any gifts. I am just happy that my brother is alive." She showed them the snake and the brick that were meant to kill her brother and explained why she had been abusing him and why she had acted so strangely during the wedding. When her parents came to know all of this, they were grateful and loving to her. "I wanted to save my brother's life and the happy marriage of my *bhaujī* (brother's wife)," she said. Her parents then sent her to her in-laws' home with great happiness, and everyone lived happily ever after.[1] (PHOOLMATI—81—SHEOLI).

27a. VARIATION ON STORY NO. 27

In this variation, the sister goes to get a pot and a rope from some carpenters, who tell her that they are making shoes for the gods and will fill them with the heart of a man whose sister has never abused him. She thus begins to abuse her brother, saying, "*Bhaiyā marai bhaujaiyā rāṅḍ hoy*" (May my brother die and my brother's wife become a widow). When they reach a river, the river says, "I will drown your brother." The sister begs, "Please don't do that. I will offer you a golden brick if you spare my brother's life." The river agrees. After a while, the sister meets a snake who says, "I will bite your brother during his *phaldān* (engagement ceremony)." She catches the snake and puts it into her bag. The sister returns home with her brother, but his feelings are hurt because she has been abusing him the whole way.

The carpenters come to take the brother's heart, but they find it full of holes from his sister's abuses, so they return empty-handed. During her brother's engagement ceremony, she insists on sitting up front, and everyone whispers that she has gone mad. When the groom's party leaves for the bride's house, she insists on going along for the marriage ceremony. When the bride and groom return home, she insists on sleeping between them. The snake comes to bite the brother as he lies with his new wife, but the sister is between them, and the snake is forced to turn away. Thus the sister saves her brother.[2] (PHOOLMATI—81—SHEOLI).

28. A BROTHER'S DANGEROUS JOURNEY TO HIS SISTER

Once there were seven sisters who had a brother who was very dear to all of them. The eldest sister, Kamladevi, was married and lived in a distant place. On the day of Bhaiyā Dūj, the brother complained to his mother, "I haven't received any sweets from my eldest sister today." His mother tried to pacify him, saying, "You can get sweets from her another time. Perhaps she will send sweets with someone today. She does live very far away." The brother insisted on going to see his sister, however, when he learned that a neighbor was going that way. Thus, the brother set off on the long journey to his sister's home.

On the way, the brother had to cross a river. As soon as he started across, the river swelled up and said, "I am going to drown you." "Why?" asked the boy. "Because you are dear to your parents and sisters," replied the river. "All right," said the brother, "you can drown me, but first let me visit my sister." The river agreed, and he continued on his way.

Before he had gone much further, the brother met a cobra who puffed out his hood and said, "I am going to bite you." "Why do you want to bite me?" asked the boy. "Because you are dear to your parents and sisters," answered the cobra. "All right, you can bite me," bargained the boy, "but let me visit my sister first." The cobra agreed, and he continued on his way.

Next he met a lion, who blocked his path and snarled, "I am going to eat you up." "Why do you want to eat me?" asked the brother. "Because you are dear to your parents and sisters," answered the lion. "All right, I will let you eat me, if I can visit my sister first." The lion agreed, and he continued on his way.

A little further on, the brother was stopped by a wolf, who growled, "I am going to eat you up." "Why do you want to eat me?" he asked. "Because you are dear to your parents and sisters," answered the wolf. "All right, I will let you eat me, if I can visit my sister first." The wolf agreed, and the boy continued on his way.

The brother finally reached his sister's home. At the moment he arrived, she was trying to join the two ends of a broken thread and could not get up to greet him. He felt insulted and thought to himself, "I have traveled a great distance and risked my life several times to come to see my sister, yet she doesn't even get up to greet me." Angrily, he turned to leave, but the sister finished joining the broken thread and pulled him back inside the house. "Why are you leaving in anger?" she asked. "I have been standing here so long, and you didn't even care to welcome me," her brother complained. "Dear brother," she soothed, "I was making preparations for your worship and I couldn't stop in the middle of them, lest some harm come to you." The sister thus calmed him, offered him sweets and milk, and asked for news of her parents, sisters, and neighbors.

Then the sister went to her neighbor to ask, "What food should I prepare for my brother, who has come for Bhaiyā Dūj?" The neighbor jokingly said, "Cook rice in ghī to make khīr and cook pūrīs in milk." The sister did as the neighbor told her, but the food tasted terrible and the brother couldn't eat it. She herself was eating yogurt and pūrīs made of chickpea flour, so she gave him some of her own food to eat.

Then her brother asked, "Sister, how much do you love me?" "As much as salt," she replied. "What?" he responded angrily, ready to leave again. "I am the only brother among seven sisters, and my eldest sister thinks I am worth only as much as salt!" "Don't get angry," his sister chided him. "Let me show you how important salt is." Thereafter she started preparing all the food with sugar instead of salt. After several days, he complained, "Sister, you are not making good food. I am hungry all the time." She answered him, "Now you understand the importance of salt and the depth of my love for you."

The night before the brother was to leave, he became very sad and couldn't eat any food at all. His sister pressed him to find out the reason for his sadness, and finally he told her about the river, the cobra, the lion, and the wolf who were waiting to take his life on the return journey. His sister consoled him, saying, "Don't worry, I will handle everything." The next morning when he was ready to leave, she gave him two large loaves of bread, barley, rice, sesame seeds, and a pot of milk. "Use these things to avert your death," she advised her brother. Thus equipped, he set off on his journey. When he met the wolf, he threw one loaf of bread to him; when he met the lion, he tossed him the other loaf; when he met the cobra, he gave him the pot of milk; and when he reached the river, he offered the barley, rice, and sesame seeds. Thus the brother escaped his adversaries and reached home safely.

After some time, brother's marriage was arranged, so the eldest sister asked her husband to give her jewelry and a sari so that she could go to her brother's wedding. During the marriage ceremony, a cobra slid up to the brother. The eldest sister rushed up and pleaded with the cobra, "Please don't bite the groom. He is my younger brother." She offered milk to the cobra, who was so pleased that he prayed, "May you be my sister in all my lives to follow."[3] (BUDDHAMATI—48—SHEOLI).

29. THE BROTHER'S BET

Once a woman's husband and brother got into a fight. The husband told the brother that he wouldn't let him set foot inside his house again, even to get rocanā from his sister on Bhaiyā Dūj. The brother vowed, "Somehow I will get rocanā from my sister on Bhaiyā Dūj. You wait and see!"

When Bhaiyā Dūj came, the brother came to his sister's house, but found all the doors locked, with the sister's husband standing guard. He could hear his sister crying inside and soon he too began to cry outside. The brother was determined to get his rocanā from her, so he transformed himself into a dog and crept into the house through the drain. There he saw his sister weeping and grinding turmeric for the worship of Bhaiyā Dūj. When she saw the dog, coming out of the drain, she threw the turmeric-stained grinding stone and hit the dog, making the mark of rocanā on its forehead.

The dog slipped back out through the drain, then transformed himself back into his original self, and showed the mark on his forehead to his sister's husband. Angrily, the husband went inside, ready to beat his wife for disobeying his orders. She swore that no one had come inside the house, "A dog crept in through the drain, but I threw my grinding stone at it and it ran away."

Then the husband understood what had happened and went back outside to berate his wife's brother. "Shame on you! You came into my house as a dog!" His brother-in-law retorted proudly, "I don't care how I went. Despite your efforts, I managed to get my rocanā from my sister on Bhaiyā Dūj." Finally the husband had to admit he had lost and his brother-in-law had won.[4] (PHOOLMATI—81—SHEOLI).

30. TELL ME WHERE YOUR LIFE RESIDES

Once a brother and sister lived with their stepmother. The sister knew that the stepmother didn't like them, so when she left for her in-laws' home, she cautioned her brother, "Don't ever tell your wife any secrets." "Why?" asked her innocent brother. "Just follow my advice," his sister warned.

When she reached her husband's home, the sister immediately filled two pots with milk and put a few *sīñk* (wickers) in them. She knew that the wickers would turn the milk red if her brother was in trouble.

At the brother's home, the stepmother began to speak badly of the brother to his wife, in an effort to turn her against him. "Your husband doesn't love you," needled the mother-in-law. "Oh, yes, he does," the wife said proudly. "If he loves you, he should tell you where his life resides," insisted the mother-in-law. Thus she planted a seed of doubt in her daughter-in-law's mind. That night the wife pestered her husband, "Tell me where your life resides. Only then will I know that you truly love me." The brother tried to dissuade his wife from asking this, but she insisted, so he lied, "My life is in the rope with which I tie the cow when I milk her."

The naive wife ran to tell this to her mother-in-law the next morning, to prove that her husband really did love her. The stepmother immediately went out and replaced the cow's rope with a snake. During the day, however, the snake turned into a black thread, which the boy found when he went to milk the cow that evening. "Whose black thread is this?" he asked his stepmother. "No one is more dear to me than yourself," lied his stepmother. Her stepson therefore put the black thread around his waist.

Inside, his stepmother was angry at being thwarted in her efforts to kill him. She approached her daughter-in-law again, saying, "I'm sure your husband doesn't love you at all. Ask him again where his life resides." Filled with doubt because of her mother-in-law's evil words, the brother's wife again begged her husband, "Tell me where your life resides. Only then will I know that you truly love me." Again her husband tried to dissuade her, but she insisted, so he told her, "My life resides in the pot that I use for milking the cow."

The next morning, the foolish wife again ran to her mother-in-law, relating this information as proof that her husband loved her. The stepmother immediately went and put a scorpion in the milking pot. During the day, however, the scorpion turned into a ring, which the brother found when he went to milk the cow. "Whose ring is this?" he asked his stepmother. "No one is more dear to me than yourself," replied his stepmother again, so he put the ring on his finger.

The stepmother was furious. The next day she taunted her daughter-in-law mercilessly, "Your husband holds no love for you in his heart at all." By the end of the day, the woman was so sad and depressed that she refused to talk to her husband. "You have lied to me! If you really loved me, you would tell me honestly where your life resides." Her poor husband got very upset and thus, against his better judgment, he told his wife the truth, "My life resides in the pond on the outskirts of this village."

Naturally, by the next morning, his stepmother knew this also. She immediately went to the pond with twigs, wood, and cowdung cakes, which she set on fire and threw into the pond. As the fire burned, her stepson became feverish.

Meanwhile, the sister saw the milk in her pots turn red and knew that her brother was in trouble. She picked up her infant son and a pot of yogurt and hurried down the road to her brother's aid. On the way, she got very tired from carrying the baby, so she had to leave him behind on the road. When the sister reached the pond, she threw her pot of yogurt on the fire and thus put it out. As the fire subsided, her brother's temperature returned to normal, so that when she reached his house, they had a happy reunion. Then she heaved a great sigh. "What is wrong?" asked her brother. "You didn't follow my advice, so I had to come and save your life. I left my baby on the road for your sake and now I fear for his safety," his sister replied.

Hearing this, the brother asked her to tell him exactly where she had left baby. He grabbed a pot of milk and ran off down the road. Soon he saw the baby, sucking his toe, while a cobra spread his hood above him. The cobra had come to protect the boy when his mother left him, because of her devotion to her brother, but the brother didn't know this and was in a dilemma as to what to do. When the snake saw him, he slid away; the brother ran to his nephew, picked him up, and gave him the milk to drink. Thus the sister's brother and son were both saved, because of the sister's deep love for her brother. (PHOOLMATI—81—SHEOLI).

31. THE SNAKE BROTHER'S REVENGE

There was once a milkmaid who had tamed some snakes which she kept under some large earthen pots. Without explaining why, she told her daughter, "Don't ever lift up these earthen pots." The daughter kept her curiosity within bounds for a long time, but one day when her mother was out selling milk, she could resist no longer. She lifted the cover of one of the earthen pots and was horrified to see many baby snakes. In fright, she dropped the pot, killing several baby snakes and cutting off one baby snake's tail. When this snake grew big enough to go out to play, he was teased by the other snakes who called him *baḍavā* (one whose tail is cut). The young snake came home in tears and asked his mother, "Why do the other snakes call me baḍavā?" "Because your tail is cut," she answered gently. "How did that happen?" pressed the young snake. His mother told him, "One day when you were just a baby, your human sister opened the pot under which you and your brothers and sisters were lying. She was so startled that she dropped the cover in haste, cutting off your tail." This made the young snake very angry. "I'm going to find her and bite her," he vowed. His mother tried to calm him, but he wouldn't listen.

Eventually the snake found his way to his human sister's house. Just then, however, his sister and her mother-in-law were in the midst of a hot argument. His sister had just finished smearing the kitchen with mud and had some drops of mud on her sari. Her mother-in-law thought they were drops of yogurt, however, and was berating her for eating yogurt on the sly. At the end of the argument, the snake's sister vowed solemnly, "By the oath of my brother Baḍavā, whom I love very much, I swear that I am telling the truth." Hearing how much his sister loved him made the snake feel ashamed of his intentions, so he returned home quietly and told his mother, "I don't want to bite my sister after all. Make preparations for me to bring her home to stay with us a while."

Then the snake went back to his sister's house, bearing all the customary gifts. The mother-in-law refused to let his sister go, however, until he threatened, "I will bite everyone in your family if you don't let my sister return home with me." Thus the snake brought his sister home.[5] (PHOOLMATI—81—SHEOLI).

32. SATANA'S SEVEN BROTHERS

Once there was a girl named Satana, who had seven brothers who loved her very much. One time all the brothers had to go away together, so each of them asked his wife to take good care of his sister. The wives all promised to watch over their sister-in-law, but as soon as the men left, their wives made her work very hard.

One brother's wife told her, "Go and milk the cows in this sieve." Poor Satana didn't know what to do, so she went to the forest and started crying, "*Sāto bhaiyā ban gaye bañajār gaye, Satānā rvāvayañ bhījhā ban me*" (My seven brothers have gone to the forest and Satana is weeping in the lonely forest). Some swans flying overhead heard her crying and came down to ask, "What is the matter?" Satana replied tearfully, "My brother's wife asked me to milk the cows in a sieve, but when I do so, the milk filters out onto the ground. I don't know what to do." "Don't worry," said one swan, "I will spread my wings and you can put your sieve on it to milk the cows. Carry me home and set me down in the open courtyard." Satana did as the swan told her. When the brother's wife came to fetch the sieve, the swan flew away.

The next day another brother's wife ordered Satana, "Take this black blanket and make it white without washing it." Again, poor Satana didn't know what to do and went crying to the forest, "My seven brothers have gone to the forest and Satana is weeping in the lonely forest." Some pigeons flew past her at that moment and asked kindly, "What is wrong?" Satana answered, "My brother's wife told me to make this black blanket white without washing it, but I don't know how to do that." "Don't worry," said the pigeons, "just spread out the blanket." Satana did so and all the pigeons defecated on it until it was completely white. Satana took it home, happy to have completed the task.

The next day another brother's wife told Satana, "Take this basket of unthreshed rice and separate the rice from the chaff." Poor Satana went to the forest crying again, "My seven brothers have gone to the forest and Satana is weeping in the lonely forest." Just then, a flock of sparrows flew by and tried to comfort her. "Why are you crying?" they asked. Satana replied, "My brother's wife told me to separate the rice from the chaff, but I don't know how to do it." The sparrows assured her, "Don't worry, we will do it for you." Thus the sparrows separated the rice and chaff with their beaks. A one-eyed sparrow who was a little greedy put half a grain of rice in her empty eye, however, when no one was looking. When Satana brought the rice home, her brother's wife counted each grain and shouted at her, "One half-grain of rice is missing. Bring it to me!" Satana returned to the forest in tears again that day. The sparrows came to her again when they heard her crying, "My brother's wife says that a half-grain of rice is missing. Please help me." The sparrows realized that the one-eyed sparrow had stolen it, so they got it from her and gave it to Satana, who was thus able to pacify her brother's wife.

The next day another brother's wife ordered Satana, "Go bring a load of wood for me, without tying a rope to it." Poor Satana went to the forest and began to cry, "My seven brothers have gone to the forest and Satana is weeping in the lonely forest." A serpent heard her and came to her aid. "What is the matter?" he hissed. "My brother's wife told me to bring a load of wood without tying a rope to it. I cannot carry a loose bundle of wood." The serpent said, "Don't worry. Gather the wood and tie me around it." Satana did as the serpent suggested, brought the wood home, and set it down near the drain, so that the serpent could escape.

The day for Bhaiyā Dūj came. Satana became very sad, thinking of her brothers who were away. She escaped to the forest and began to weep, "My seven brothers have gone to the forest and Satana is weeping in the lonely forest."

At that very moment, her brothers were on their way home, anxious that they should not miss Bhaiyā Dūj. As they passed through the forest, the eldest brother said to the others, "I hear some crying. It sounds like Satana." The other brothers reasoned with him, "Why would Satana be here in the forest? She must be at home relaxing." They continued on their way, but before long, the eldest brother heard the crying again. "I'm sure I hear Satana crying," he insisted. The other brothers began to tease him, "You are just thinking of her a lot. That is why you think you hear her crying." The eldest brother became adamant, "We must go find her!" Finally he convinced the others, and they searched the forest until they found Satana sitting under a tree weeping.

"Deat sister," they exclaimed in distress, "why are you sitting in the forest crying?" Satana then told her brothers how their wives had mistreated her and they swore to take revenge. The eldest brother opened his thigh and hid Satana inside.

When they reached home, the brothers asked their wives, "Where is Satana?" Each wife made up a lie, such as, "She was just here combing her hair," "She was just outside taking a bath," "She was just now eating khīr," or "She went to lie down." None of the wives could find Satana, however. Then the elder brother took Satana out of his thigh, and Satana accused all her brother's wives of mistreating her. Her sisters-in-law were very ashamed and begged their husbands for forgiveness, but the brothers boiled oil in a big pot and sprinkled it over their wives in punishment for their behavior towards Satana.[6] (MAYA SHUKLA—32—PATTI).

33. BROTHER VISITS TWO SISTERS

Once there lived a brother who had seven sisters who loved him very much. On the day of Bhaiyā Dūj, the brother went to his eldest sister's house. She was very happy and went to ask her neighbor, "What shall I make for my beloved brother on Bhaiyā Dūj?" The neighbor thought she was joking and told her, "Fry the rice in milk and then boil it in butter to make *khīr*." The sister was so excited that her brother had come that she didn't think twice about her neighbor's instructions and followed them exactly. The poor brother tried hard to eat the khīr, because he didn't want to hurt his sister's feeling, but eventually he had to admit, "I can't eat any more, because the rice is so hard." Meanwhile, the neighbor came to meet the brother and realized that the sister had followed her silly instructions. Then she showed her the proper way to make khīr, and brother and sister ate happily together.

After a few hours, the brother took his leave, so that he could visit his second sister. As it happens, she was just on her way to his house and they met on the road. "Where are you going?" asked the brother. "To put tilak on your forehead," answered the second sister. She put the mark on his forehead and both were very happy.

Then the brother said, "I must go and join a marriage party today." The sister prayed, "May my brother be safe from thorns while going through the jungle with the marrige party." The brother left, but on his way, he got badly stuck with thorns. When his second sister learned of this, she came to his aid despite the burning summer heat. All the members of the marriage party were impressed by her love and devotion.

When the brother returned home, his wife asked him, "How did you enjoy Bhaiyā Dūj today?" With happiness and pride, her husband told her everything that had happened that day. The wife sniffed, "Your sisters are crazy," "No, they're not," retorted her husband. "My sisters are gentle and soft-hearted." "Humph," said the wife, "I will make khīr for you, as it should be made." She did so, but when her husband ate it, he commented, "Your khīr doesn't have the good taste that my sister's khīr had." (BHAGWATI PANDEY—57—KANPUR CITY).

34. AN INTERCASTE MARRIAGE CONTRACT

Once upon a time, there was a king's family and a sweeper's family. It happend that both the queen and the sweeper woman were pregnant. One day while the sweeper woman and the queen were talking about their expected times of delivery, they jokingly agreed that if they gave birth to children of opposite sexes, their offspring would be married. Eventually the sweeper woman gave birth to a boy and the queen to a girl. When they came of age, the sweeper woman said, "It is time for them to get married." The queen became very upset as to what to do. On the day of Bhaiyā Dūj, the queen asked her daughter to make preparations for the special day. She had her go immediately to the sweeper's house and put the mark of Bhaiyā Dūj on the son's forehead. "That way you won't have to marry a sweeper," said the queen. The daughter performed the worship of Bhaiyā Dūj and immediately went to the sweeper's house, where she found the boy lying on a cot. She put the mark of Bhaiyā Dūj on his forehead and he got up and touched her feet; she asked for a present and he gave it to her—thus the queen's daughter and the sweeper woman's son became brother and sister. The sweeper woman watched helplessly, realizing that her plan for her son's royal marriage had been foiled. (MAHADEVI —70—KANPUR CITY).

NOTES

1. See Sita 1970:51. A similar story was recorded from Mahadevi—70—Kanpur city.
2. See Pandey 1967:197 and Tripathi 1977:471. A similar story was recorded from Bhagwati Shukla—54—Varanasi.
3. See Pandey 1967:198. Similar stories were recorded from Bhagwati Shukla—54—Varanasi and Beti Devi—85—Sheoli.
4. See Pandey 1967:193. Similar stories were recorded from Bhagwati Pandey—57—Kanpur city and Bhagwati Shukla—54—Varanasi.
5. See Pandey 1967:139.
6. See "Ta'pai" in Mohanti 1975:83, "Sakkar Bahan" and "Birana Bai" in Parmar 1969:341 and 1975:181; and Tripathi 1977:482. A similar story was recorded from Mahadevi—70—Kanpur city.

Plate 9. Bhaiyā Dūj
A floor painting, with rice paste, showing the sun and moon, a sieve, a snake, a tulsī plant, twigs of *bhaṭakaṭaiyā* (a prickly shrub), an animal, Ganga-Yamuna, bowls full of sweets, a stone slab and muller, a sister, seven brothers, and aravals. (Sheela Pandey—26—Kanpur city).

XI. KARVĀ CAUTH

On the fourth day of the bright half of Kārtik, Karvā Cauth is observed by all married women to ensure the long lives and good health of their husbands. Women fast all day long, without taking even water. It is customary for a woman to receive a *karvā* (an earthen pot with a spout) and presents from her parents' family on this day. Pua, pūrī, *pinnī, kaḍhi, pharā,* and *ciuḍā* are specially made. Some of the food is put in one karvā, and water in another. During the day, a colorful painting is made on the wall (see Plate 10);[1] in the evening all women observing the fast tell stories and worship the painting with their two karvās. When the moon appears, the women say prayers and offer the food and water. Only after they have worshipped Gauri and the moon do they eat or drink anything.[2]

35. THE GLUTTONOUS WIFE

Once there lived a husband and wife. On the day of Karvā Cauth, the wife said to her husband, "Bring a new lahañgā and dupattā for me because it is Karvā Cauth, and I will fast until evening." The husband promised to bring what his wife requested, but then went and hid himself on the roof of the house. From his hiding place he watched her go out to relieve herself in the fields and then eat some sugarcane. When she came home, she fried some grain on the iron griddle and ate it. Then, she made some pūrīs and *pakauḍī* and ate them also. Her husband realized, "She pretends to be fasting, but she eats a lot in secret."

After a while, the wife started to churn the buttermilk. When the *nenū* (butter) came to the top, she rolled it into a ball and began to toss it in the air, saying, "*Kahau nenū gaṭṭakau kī nā gaṭṭakau?*" (Say, should I eat this butter or not?) Answering herself, she replied, "*Gaṭṭakau gaṭṭakau*" (Eat, eat), and popped the butter into her mouth.

Then her husband came down from the roof with a stick in his hand and said, "*Kahau ḍaṅḍā caṭṭakai ki nā caṭṭakai?*" (Should the stick strike or not?) Not knowing why he was saying this, the bewildered wife answered, "*Caṭṭakai caṭṭakai*" (Strike, strike), and her husband began to beat her for lying about fasting. (RAMKALI MISRA—62—SHEOLI).

35a. VARIATION ON STORY NO. 35

In this variation, the woman asks her husband for a new lahaṅgā and dupaṭṭā for Karvā Cauth. The husband agrees, but goes and hides himself on the roof of the house to spy on his wife's activities. Thinking that her husband is gone, the wife makes pūrīs, fries a piece of fish, and eats heartily. Then she parches some grain to munch on and chews sugarcane. When her husband returns that evening, without the items she requested, the wife complains, "I fasted the whole day, and now I cannot perform the worship." The husband tells her, "Never mind. Prepare the worship without the new lahaṅgā and dupaṭṭā, and I will tell the story." The wife thus begins the worship, while her husband recites:

Sunau Gaur jī pūjā.	Listen to the worship of Gaur.
Ek uṅkh paravāṅā	First you ate sugarcane.
Soharī aiso kānā.	Then you ate soharī.
Ūpar mīn ko khāṅḍā,	Still hungry you ate fish
paraī bharbhūṅjā.	and grains.
Lev Gaur a\v pūjā.	Receive this offering, Oh, Gaur.

Then the husband beats his deceitful wife.[3] (BETI DEVI—85—SHEOLI).

36. PRINCESS OVERCOMES SPINSTERHOOD

Once there was a king's daughter who wanted to get married. A *sañyāsī* (ascetic) who came to the palace one day looked at her palm and told her that she was not destined to be married. "Is there any way I can change my fate?" asked the unhappy girl. "Yes, there is one way," replied the sañyāsī. "If you serve a *dhobin* (washerwoman) for twelve years, you will get a husband."

The king's daughter therefore began to serve a dhobin secretly. At midnight she would arise and go to the dhobin's house to clean her pots and pans, mop her house, and clean her stable. The dhobin began to wonder, "Who serves me so faithfully, without my knowing them?" One night she hid herself and stayed awake to see who did the work during the night. Shortly after midnight, the king's daughter arrived and began to work. The dhobin seized her and demanded, "Why are you performing these services for me?" The girl begged her, "Please let me go. I promise that I will not come again." The dhobin insisted on knowing the reason for her service, however, and the girl finally bargained, "If I tell you why I have been coming here, will you give me whatever I ask of you?" "Yes," promised the dhobin.

"I am not destined to be married," sighed the king's daughter, "but I wish it very much. A sañyāsī told me that I could change my fate if I served a dhobin for twelve years; that is why I have been serving you. Now put señdur in the part of my hair."

"You have asked too much," replied the dhobin, "but I will give you what I promised." Then the dhobin applied señdur to the girl's part. As soon as she did so, her own husband died, but the dhobin cut the little finger of her left hand and sprinkled blood over his body and he came back to life.[4] (RAMKALI—62—SHEOLI).

37. SATTO AND THE FALSE MOON

Once a girl named Satto lived with her seven brothers and their wives. All the brothers loved their sister very much and were constantly concerned about her welfare. On the day of Karvā Cauth, Satto fasted along with all her brothers' wives, despite the fact that her brothers had tried to persuade her not to fast, because they worried she would get too hungry if she passed the whole day without food or water. When evening fell, one brother climbed up a baragad tree, carrying a lamp, which he covered with a sieve to make it look like the moon. The other brothers told Satto that she should get ready for her worship, and pointed out the "moon" in the tree. Satto made her offerings and worshipped the "moon" held by her brother, thinking that it was the real thing; then she broke her fast by drinking water and eating some food.

Just then, a messenger came from her husband's home, saying, "Your husband has just died." Everyone became sad and wondered how this could have happened, since her husband had been in excellent health when Satto left. Then the brothers' wives told their husbands, "Satto worshipped your fake moon; that is why this misfortune has befallen her." All the brothers were in great distress. "What can we do to counteract this event?" they wailed. Their wives told them, "Keep your sister's husband's body in a safe place until a year has passed. On Karvā Cauth, Satto must fast and worship the real moon; then her husband will come back to life."

Thus Satto's husband's body was kept in a room, where she cared for it faithfully for one year. On the day of Karvā Cauth, she fasted, made offerings, and worshipped the moon. As soon as she finished the worship, her husband came back to life.

Since then, all Hindu women have observed Karvā Cauth. They fast all day long, without taking even water; only after they have worshipped the moon will they eat or drink anything.[5] (BHAGWATI PANDEY—57—KANPUR CITY).

38. COBRA BROTHER BRINGS PRESENTS

Once there was a woman who had no brothers. On the day of Karvā Cauth, she heard the other women at the well bragging about the presents they had received from their parents' home for the occasion. The woman felt sad and left out and thought, "If I had a brother, I also would have received a karvā today." Her mother-in-law and sister-in-law came along and teased her about this, and soon she began to weep quietly at the well.

A cobra who lived near the well heard all of this. He went to his mother and told her, "Prepare a karvā and everything that goes with it, so that I can take it to my sister's home." "What sister are you talking about?" asked his mother. "I have a *dharm-kī-bahan* (sister-by-religion)," replied the cobra. His mother then put a karvā in a cart and piled the cart high with presents as well as all the ingredients for the worship of Karvā Cauth. The cobra slithered down the road with the cart following him.

When the cobra reached the woman's house, he transformed himself into a young man and informed her in-laws, "I am your daughter-in-law's brother and have come with presents for Karvā Cauth." At first her in-laws said, "She doesn't have a brother," but the cobra-man insisted, "I am her elder brother." When they saw the wonderful presents he had brought, the woman's mother-in-law, sister-in-law, and other family members began to respect her, and everyone praised her brother. In the evening, the woman performed the worship of the moon with a golden karvā which had a silver lid. (BHAGWATI PANDEY—57—KANPUR CITY).

39. REWARD MATCHES DEVOTION

Once there was a boy who earned two paisā each day. He used to give one paisā to his mother and spend the other paisā on flowers to offer in Ganesh*ji*'s temple. Another boy also earned two paisā a day, but he gave them both to his mother.

One day the first boy's mother asked him, "Why do you give me only one paisā a day, when you earn two? Your friend gives both of his paisā to his mother." "I use one paisā to worship Ganesh*ji*," replied the boy humbly. Angrily, the mother spurned him, "Then go to Ganesh*ji* and ask him for food. I have nothing to feed you." The boy fled to the temple in tears. Ganesh*ji* appeared and asked, "Why are you crying?" The boy wept, "My mother said I should come ask you for food, since I spend one paisā on flowers for you every day." Ganesh*ji* spoke kindly to the boy, "Gather all the flowers and leaves that have been offered here and take them to your mother." The boy did as he was told, but when he laid the flowers and leaves at his mother's feet, they turned into gold, silver and precious stones, by the grace of Ganesh*ji*. On seeing this, the mother blessed her son and asked his forgiveness.

When the mother of the other boy heard about this miracle, she told her son to start offering flowers to Ganesh*ji* in the same manner. There was a big difference between the two boys, however. The second boy spent only half a paisā on flowers, using the other half paisā to buy sweets for himself, although he told his mother he was offering one paisā's worth of flowers to Ganesh*ji* every day. After a while, the second mother did as the first had done, sending her son to ask Ganesh*ji* for food. When the boy came crying to the temple, Ganesh*ji* appeared; as with the first boy, Ganesh*ji* told him to take the leaves and flowers of the temple to his mother, but when he laid these in front of her, they turned into snakes and scorpions. The second mother came to Ganesh*ji* to complain about their inequitable treatment. Ganesh*ji* told her, "Dedication is rewarded, not mere show."[7] (BHAGWATI PANDEY—57—KANPUR CITY).

40. THE TALKING TREE

One day a *Nanad* (husband's sister) asked her *Bhābhī* (brother's wife) to give her a sari so that she could go with her friends to bathe in the river. "No," said Bhābhī, "you will ruin it." Nanad insisted, however, and Bhābhī finally gave in. At the river, Nanad wrapped the sari in her friends' saris to protect it while she was bathing, but an eagle spotted her sari and urinated on it. Nanad came home crying with the soiled sari. When Bhābhī heard what had happened, she was so angry that she went straight to her room and stayed there until her husband came home. He tried to console her, but she complained, "My head is aching. I will be cured only after you have killed your sister and dyed my sari in her blood." Her husband tried to dissuade her, but Bhābhī was adamant.

Sadly, the brother took his sister outside and asked her to wait while he climbed a *ber* tree. "Take these bers which I have picked for you." Nanad stretched out her hands, but her brother said, "No, not in your hands." Nanad spread out her sari, but her brother said, "No, not in your sari." Then Nanad opened her mouth and her brother cut out her tongue with his knife, whereupon she died. On the spot where she died, a beautiful tree grew up.

A year later, a barbar from Nanad's in-laws' house came to make arrangements for her *gaunā* (a marriage ceremony). Standing under that tree, he was so overwhelmed by its beauty that he wanted to smell the leaves. When he tried to pluck a leaf, however, a voice said:

> *Sasure ke nauvā pat jani chuvau, pat jani chuvau;*
> *Bhaiyā mārai bhaujī oḍhai, raktā kā boro cīr.*
> Oh barber from my in-laws house, do not touch my leaves;
> My brother has killed me, to dye his wife's sari in my blood, so she can wear it.

The barber went back and related this to Nanad's in-laws. The *bārī* (a caste among Hindus who prepare and sell plates and cups made of leaves) was sent. He also tried to pick the leaves of the beautiful tree, but it said:

> *Sasure ke bariyā pat jani chuvau, pat jani chuvau;*

Bhaiyā mārai bhaujī oḍhai, raktā kā boro cīr.
Oh bari from my in-laws house, do not touch my leaves;
My brother has killed me, to dye his wife's sari in my blood, so she can wear it.

The bārī went back and related this to Nanad's in-laws. Nanad's *devar* (husband's younger brother) came next; he too was warned not to touch the tree:

Devar hamāre pat jani chuvau, pat jani chuvau;
Bhaiyā mārai bhaujī oḍhai, raktā kā boro cīr.
Oh my devar, do not touch my leaves;
My brother has killed me, to dye his wife's sari in my blood, so she can wear it.

When Nanad's jeth came, the tree said:

Jeṭh hamāre pat jani chuvau, pat jani chuvau;
Bhaiyā mārai bhaujī oḍhai, raktā kā boro cīr.
Oh my jeth, do not touch my leaves;
My brother has killed me, to dye his wife's sari in my blood, so she can wear it.

Concerned over this situation, Nanad's sasur came to see the tree, which beseeched him:

Sasur hamāre pat jani chuvau, pat jani chuvau;
Bhaiyā mārai bhaujī oḍhai, raktā kā boro cīr.
Oh my sasur, do not touch my leaves;
My brother has killed me, to dye his wife's sari in my blood, so she can wear it.

Finally Nanad's husband came to see for himself; the tree addressed him:

Svāmī hamāre pat jani chuvau, pat jani chuvau;
Bhaiyā mārai bhaujī oḍhai, raktā kā boro cīr.
Oh my husband, do not touch my leaves;
My brother has killed me, to dye his wife's sari in my blood, so she can wear it.

This made her husband so angry that he pulled the tree apart.

As soon as the tree was broken, Nanad appeared alive before him. He then sent a message to her house, "Make preparations for the gaunā." Hearing this, the brother felt very worried, because he knew he had killed his sister. When the sister arrived with her husband, the brother asked for forgiveness and sent her off to her husband's home.[8] (BETI DEVI—85—SHEOLI).

41. FOUR FRAUDULENT BROTHERS

There once were four brothers who returned from a long stay abroad after making a good fortune. None of them was married. They decided to obtain a wife by deceitful means. "1000-1200 rupees should accomplish our goal," they reasoned. In the neighboring village, they spied on a woman who had no brothers. On the day of Karvā Cauth, they came to her in-laws' house, bringing a cartload of presents. The in-laws took the presents greedily and told the daughter-in-law, "Your brothers have come." The daughter-in-law protested, "I have never seen these men before." The would-be brothers lied, "Dear sister, you were very young when we left for abroad; now that we have returned with riches, we have come to see you and bring you home." The daughter-in-law did not believe them and was not willing to go with them, but her father-in-law reasoned, "They have brought so many presents; if you go with them, we will receive many more. You must go." Thus the woman's in-laws forced her to leave with the men.

On the road, birds kept warning her, singing, "Daughter-in-law, these are thieves who are carrying you." The daughter-in-law not understanding what the birds were saying, asked the men, "Brothers, what are these birds saying?" The fraudulent brothers answered, "They are not saying anything, keep quiet!" The daughter-in-law kept asking them, however, and told them, "I think the birds are calling you 'thieves'." By this time, they had travelled some distance, so they said, "Keep quiet, we have spent enough money to get you." Helplessly, the daughter-in-law was silent. After a while, she pleaded, "I need to make a bowel movement." The men stopped the cart and told her to go into the fields. As soon as the daughter-in-law reached a field of *arahar (citisus cajan)*, she took off her jewelry and outer garments and hid them in a pit; wearing only her underskirt and blouse, she began plucking chickpea greens. When the daughter-in-law didn't come back for a long time, the four men began to search for her. Seeing a woman plucking chickpea greens, they asked, "Have you seen a woman here?" She responded, "Yes, there was a woman here a while ago, but she ran off in that direction." The four false brothers immediately went running off to look for her.

The daughter-in-law returned to the outskirts of her village and sat on a swing in a garden. Many days passed. Her husband was uneasy, for whenever he went near the place, he thought, "That is my own wife swinging in the garden." One day, able to bear it no longer, the husband called her name and begged her to return home. She answered, "I won't come back, because your family sent me away with thieves!" The husband persisted in pleading with her, however, and persuaded her to come home with him. (MAHADEVI—70—KANPUR CITY).

NOTES

1. See also Marriott 1955:205.
2. Wiser (1971:33–34) mentions that this festival is observed by Muslim women as well. "At the time of *Karva Chaut*, when Hindu wives seek the favor of the gods for the prosperity of their husbands by fasting and by special drawings on their walls, the Muslim women do likewise." See Khare (1976:139–42) for details regarding food preparation and rituals. Lewis (1965:239), in his study of Rampur village, states that "Karva Cauth is observed only by Brahman, Baniya, and Kumhar women—not by Jats." Sinha (1976:45) mentions that "*Karwa Chauth* is celebrated on the 4th day of *Kartika*, for the longevity of the husbands by married (Dhanuk) women only."
3. See Pandey 1967:142 and "The Watchful Jat" in Bahadur 1972:17–18. Similar stories were recorded from Bhagwati Pandey—57—Kanpur city and Mahadevi—70—Kanpur city.
4. Two informants, Bhagwati Pandey—57—Kanpur city and Mahadevi—70—Kanpur city told similar stories for the fast of *Somvārī amāvasyā* (when the moonless night falls on a Monday). Mahadevi calls it *Somvārī pīpal*. See also Pandey 1967:297 and Khare 1976:201.
5. See Lewis 1965:217; Marriott 1955:204; Pandey 1967:138; and Sita 1970:59. In a similar story, told by Bhagwati Shukla—54—Varanasi, the sister is not named. After worshipping the fake moon and breaking her fast, the sister tells her brothers' wives that they should worship too, but they reply jealously, "Your moon has risen because you are so dear to your brothers, but our moon has not yet risen." When the news of their sister's husband's death comes, the brothers are very upset, but a divine voice tells them to keep the body safe for a year, while their sister fasts and worships on the cauths of the next twelve months. All this is done, and the sister's husband comes back to life as soon as she finishes the worship of Karvā Cauth the next year.

6. See Pandey 1967:139.
7. The informant said that this story about Ganesh*ji* could be told on Karvā Cauth, as well as at other times.
8. See "Kanchan" in Mohanti 1975:73; Sharma 1972:38; and Marzac 1977:397–413.

Plate 10. Karvā Cauth
A colorful wall painting, showing a potter woman carrying a basket full of karvās, a tulsī plant, five brothers,a sieve, God Ganesh flanked by the sun and moon, a peacock, a woman, a toy, a comb, Ganga-Yamuna, the sister and two brothers (one holding the ladder while the other shows the sieve), two karvās, an oil lamp, five lumps of mud representing Garui, a svastik, and a flower. In the center of the altar is a figure representing Karvā. (Rani Misri—34—Delhi).

XII. BAḌĪ EKĀDAŚĪ

Baḍī Ekādaśī (also known as Devṭhānī Ekādaśī) is a ritual to celebrate the awakening of the gods. According to religious belief, the gods sleep from the eleventh day of the bright half of Asāḍh to the eleventh day of the bright half of Kārtik. During these four months (known as *cāturmās*) no important new projects are begun. Only after the celebration of the gods' awakening do Indian villagers undertake auspicious work.

The household is swept and mopped clean for this celebration. Rice paste is used to make a floor painting of Vishnu's foot, and circles on which a tulsī plant is placed nearby; seven lines are drawn from the painting to the tulsī plant (see Plates 11 and 12). The household throne of deities is placed on a pāṭā on top of the floor painting. The deities and the tulsī plant are worshipped with special offerings of yams, siṅghāḍā, and sugarcane. Thereafter the throne of the deities is placed on seven pieces of sugarcane and the children of the family carry this sugarcane palanquin to the tulsī plant and back seven times to symbolize the marriage of Lord Vishnu and Tulsī. Those who fast on this day eat only yams, potatoes, and pūrīs made of siṅghāḍā flour.

Plate 11. Baḍi Ekādasī
A floor painting, made with rice paste, depicting the sun and moon, the feet of God Vishnu, fruits, a svastik, and Ganga-Yamuna. Seven lines connect the square to the tulsī plant. (Sheela Pandey—26—Kanpur city).

Plate 12. Baḍi Ekāsdasī
An intricate floor painting (very different in style from Plate 11), made with rice paste and depicting the sun and moon, a tulsī plant, svastiks, Ganga-Yamuna, flowers, and God Ganesh. In the center of the circle, surrounded by seven squares, are the feet of God Vishnu. (Suman Pandey—30—Kanpur city).

XIII. SAKAṬH

Sakaṭh or Sakaṭh *Caturthī* (fourth) is a fast observed by married women, on the fourth day of the dark half of Māgh, to protect their husbands and children and to assure the wealth and happiness of their family. Many informants told me that Sakaṭh is just another name for Ganesh*ji*. Ganesh Cauth and Sakaṭh fall on the same day, and thus these two festivals are considered one by many people. Nevertheless, the worship of Mother Sakaṭh is a separate fast in the area of my research.

Special food is prepared for the worship: *laḍḍū* (small balls) made of parched grain mixed with guḍ syrup, sweet balls of fried black and white sesame seeds, sweet potatoes, pūrīs, and *āsai*. Ghī is used to draw five human figures on a pāṭā, and a goat is molded out of black sesame seeds and guḍ syrup. (In the olden days, my informants told me, it was customary to sacrifice a live he-goat.) All of the food prepared is offered to the human figures on the pāṭā, and stories are told (see Plates 13, 14, and 15). The sesame seed goat is offered *dūrvā* grass, flowers, and a few coins; then the son of the family cuts off the goat's head, bleating as he does so. The money and the head of the sesame seed goat are given to the boy—only boys of the household are permitted to eat the goat's head.

If something auspicious has happened in the family during the year (such as a boy's marriage or the birth of a male child), all the ingredients for the worship of Sakaṭh are doubled (e.g., two sesame seed goats are made, or one from sesame seeds and one from flour) and some of the sweet is distributed to relatives and neighbors. This practice is called *Koḍvār*.

42. PARVATI AND HER SON GANESH*JI*

One day Parvati applied ubṭan to her body and made a doll's image out of the ubṭan rubbings. Then she sprinkled some nectar from her little finger onto the image and it came to life. She called him Vinayak and treated him as her son.

One day Parvati told Vinayak, "Guard the gate so that I can finish my worship undisturbed." After a little while, Shankar*ji* came to the gate and said to the boy, "Step aside, I want to go in." The boy refused him entrance, saying, "My mother is worshipping and she has asked me to guard the gate." Shankar*ji* tried to convince the boy to let him in, but was unsuccessful. In anger, he cut off the boy's head with his trident.

When Shankar*ji* entered the house, Parvati asked him where her son Vinayak was. Shankar*ji* answered, "*Mūḍ kāṭ Jamlok paṭhāyoṅ, tab ham ghar āvan pāyoṅ*" (I sent his head to Yamlok and thus managed to come inside). Hearing this, Parvati wailed, "Then cut off my head, too!" Unable to assuage her grief, Shankar*ji* suggested, "Fast and worship Mother Saṅkaṭhā.[1] Make āsai in the month of Agahan; eat four of them and give one to a Brahman. Make *khicaḍī* (a dish prepared with rice and lentils) on the month of Pūs; eat four spoonfuls of it and give one spoonful to a Brahman. Make *tilkuṭ* (sweets prepared with sesame seeds) in the month of Māgh; eat four of them and give one to a Brahman. Fry *kasār* (wheat meal fried in ghī and mixed with sugar) in the month of Phāgun. Then your son Vinayak will come back to life." Parvati did all of this, just as Shankar*ji* told her. As she was frying the kasār, her son came back to life.

Still, Parvati was distressed to see her son without a head. "Please do something," she begged her husband. Shankar*ji* said, "Go find a baby whose mother is lying with her back to it. Then bring me that baby's head." Parvati searched far and wide, but everywhere she looked she found mothers with their babies next to their breasts. Finally she saw a she-elephant sleeping, while her baby played on her back. Parvati brought the baby elephant's head to Shankar*ji*, who affixed it to Vinayak's body. Thenceforward Parvati's son was known as Ganesh*ji*.

Parvati still felt sad, however, because she thought how bad the mother elephant must feel to have her baby taken away from her. Shankar*ji* then put the head of Geṅgaṭā[2] on the baby elephant and blessed the Geṅgaṭā to live without a head forevermore.[3] (BETI DEVI—85—SHEOLI).

42a. VARIATION ON STORY NO. 42

Once Mahadev left Parvati and went to meditate for twelve years.

Parvati was very lonely. One day, after applying ubṭan to her body, she made a baby's figure out of the ubṭan rubbings, sprinkled some blood from her left finger over the figure, and lo! the baby came to life. Thus Parvati created a son, Man Vinayak, to keep her company in her husband's absence.

Years went by. One day Parvati asked her son, now twelve years old, to guard the main gate of the house while she took a bath. While she was bathing, Mahadev returned home, having finished his meditation. Man Vinayak would not let him inside the house, however, so they began to fight. Mahadev angrily cut off the boy's head with his trident.

When Parvati saw Mahadev enter the house without any warning, she wondered what happened to her son and ran out to look for him. "What are you looking for?" asked her husband. "My son, Man Vinayak," cried Parvati, "whom I asked to guard the house while I was bathing." Unaware of the creation, Mahadev stormed, "Who is this Man Vinayak?" Parvati told him how she had made a baby from her ubṭan rubbings and given it life, and thus managed to assuage the loneliness of Mahadev's long absence. Sorrowfully, Mahadev told her that he had just killed the boy.

In repentence, he told Parvati that she could bring her son back to life by fasting and worshipping on the cauths of Baisākh, Bhādau, Agahan, and Māgh. Parvati therefore fasted on these four cauths; just as she was about to perform the worship for Māgh Cauth, Man Vinayak came to life and hugged her from behind.[4] (BHAGWATI PANDEY—57—KANPUR CITY).

43. THE CHILDLESS KING

Once there lived a king who had no children. One morning when the king was sitting outside, a sweeper woman passed by and remarked, "God knows how the day will pass, since I have seen the face of the childless king." The king was upset to realize that a lowly sweeper woman could speak so rudely to him, a king, just because he was childless. He felt so depressed that he went back to bed again.

When the maidservant saw the king sleeping very late, she told him it was time to get up. "Leave me alone. I don't feel well," replied the king. The maidservant insisted on knowing what was wrong, and the king finally told her what the sweeper woman had said. Hearing this, the maidservant lied, "You don't have any reason to be sad, for your queen is already pregnant." The king didn't believe her, but the maidservant promised him, "Nine months from now, you will have a son."

From that time onward, the maidservant managed to keep the queen out of the king's sight. After nine months, the maidservant announced, "The king has been blessed with a son." Naturally the king wanted to see the child, but the maidservant told him that it would be inauspicious for him to look at the child until the *chaṭhī* was performed. The chaṭhī was celebrated with great rejoicing. When the feast was over, the king again asked to see his son, but the maidservant persuaded him to wait until the child's *barahoñ*. After the ceremony was over, the maidservant told the king to wait until the next ceremony; in this way passed the imaginary child's *pasanī, muñḍan*, and *chedan* ceremonies. The janeū ceremony presented the problem of bringing the child before the altar, but the clever maidservant told the priest and the king that the child could not appear in public; the janeū would have to be performed with the queen and the child sitting behind a curtain. After the ceremony, the maidservant again put the king off and told him he would have to wait until the boy's marriage to see him.

When girls' marriage envoys came to see the boy, the king told them that they could see only his sword and his turban. Eventually a marriage was arranged. When the marriage party left for the bride's house, the queen was distraught, thinking that the king would kill both her and the maidservant when he learned that his son did not exist. The maidservant was in command of the situation, however, and molded the image of a boy out of 1½ *man* (a unit of weight) of sesame seeds, mixed with ghī and guḍ. She put the image into the palanquin decorated for the occasion and got in herself; then the marriage party departed.

On the way to the bride's house, the groom's party stopped for the night near the temple of goddess Sakaṭh. The maidservant insisted that the palanquin be set inside the temple itself. During the night, the sweet smell of the sesame seeds, ghī and guḍ aroused the hunger of the goddess, who gobbled up the image of the boy while the maidservant was praying and making the rounds of the temple. Peeking through the window holes as she walked, the maidservant saw Goddess Sakaṭh eating the sesame seed image. She ran inside and declared, "*Leṭā khāy to beṭā dev nahīñ to sāre nagar mā thukaibe ki chaṭṭo, chaṭṭo devī*" (You must give me a son in return for eating the image, otherwise I will tell the whole city that you are a greedy goddess who loves to eat). The seven sisters[5] started accusing each other of eating the image, but finally agreed to give the maidservant a beautiful son, twelve years of age, dressed in marriage clothes.

When the boy was produced, the maidservant hurried to the king and told him he could see his son at long last. Gazing upon the chid's beauty, the king fainted. When he regained consciousness, he said, "Now I know why you waited so long to show him to me."

The marriage was performed with great happiness on both sides. When the groom's party returned home with the bride, the maidservant ran ahead to tell the queen to prepare for the welcoming ceremony. At first the queen thought that the maidservant was making fun of her, but when she heard the whole story, she was overjoyed and could hardly wait to see her son. Upon the prince's arrival, the queen bowed to the maidservant and then performed the *parachan.*[6] (BHAGWATI PANDEY—57—KANPUR CITY).

43a. VARIATION ON STORY NO. 43

This story begins like the preceding story, but differs with regard to details of the marriage party's overnight stay.

Tents were set up in a certain area. The maidservant sat alone in one tent with the sesame seed image, thinking, "Tomorrow is the wedding. What is going to happen then?"

A cobra couple lived near the place where the maidservant's tent was pitched. Attracted by the music, they wanted to have a look at the marriage party, so they entered the maidservant's tent. The cobra decided to bite the king's son, but when he bit the sesame seed image, he realised that it was not human. "What is happening here?" he thought. He returned to his wife and told her, "The one who is about to be married is made of sesame seeds." The maidservant overheard their conversation, so she told the cobra couple the whole story, begging them to help her.

"If my wife permits," offered the cobra, "I can change myself into a man." "All right," said the she-cobra, "but only if you promise to come back to me after the marriage. If you don't return, I will come and bite the princess!" The cobra promised to do as his wife asked, and then transformed himself into a handsome man. The next day the maidservant called for an elephant and told the king that he could finally see his son. When people in the marriage party saw the prince, they were very happy; the king's joy knew no bounds.

Upon the completion of the marriage ceremonies, the party set off on their return journey, camping at the same place where they had camped before. During the night, the she-cobra came to the tent where the newlyweds were lying and reminded the cobra-prince of his promise. The cobra-prince said, "I am ready to keep my promise to you, but if I leave now, it will break the hearts of the king and queen, the maidservant, and this beautiful young bride. Why don't I go to their palace with them? As soon as they are settled, I will come back." The she-cobra reluctantly agreed to let him go.

When the wedding party arrived at the palace, there was great rejoicing and the people were happy to see their handsome prince at last. The cobra-prince began to enjoy the comforts of palace life and soon forgot his promise to his cobra wife. After waiting a very long time, the she-cobra decided to take revenge; she came to the palace and bit the princess. The cobra-prince saw this happen and followed the she-cobra back to her hole, where she started to hit her head on a stone. The cobra-prince asked, "Why did you bite the princess?" The she-cobra answered, "She took my husband away from me, so I killed her, hoping that I could get him back." The cobra-prince hedged, "What you have done is justified, because I didn't keep my promise to you, but you must realize that I am in an awkward situation. I can't leave the princess even now."

The she-cobra wailed, "I knew this would happen! That is why I am killing myself, by hitting my hood upon this rock." She struck her hood upon the rock until she died. The princess came back to life as soon as the she-cobra died, and the prince and princess lived together happily for many years. (SUKHRANI DEVI—70—SHEOLI).

44. THE REWARD FOR SINCERE HOSPITALITY

Once there was a rich Devarānī and a poor Jeṭhānī. Every day Jeṭhānī went to Devarānī's house to work as a servant; in return, she received one *seer* (a unit of weight) of broken rice and a pot of buttermilk.

On the day of Sakaṭh, Jeṭhānī always fasted and made sweet balls of broken rice and *bathuā* greens to offer to the goddess. One Sakaṭh night, Goddess Sakaṭh came to Jeṭhānī and said, "I am hungry." Jeṭhānī replied, "Whatever I have is under the plate; you are welcome to it." Sakaṭh ate her fill and then said, "I need to make a bowel movement." Jeṭhānī answered, "The whole house is clean; you can defecate wherever you wish." After a while the goddess called out, "More is coming, but there is no place for it." Jeṭhānī said, "You can defecate on my head if you wish."

When Jeṭhānī woke up the next morning, she found heaps of gold all over her house. She busied herself in storing it, but this made her late for work at Devarānī's house. Devarānī came by to see what was detaining her and saw the great quantity of gold which Jeṭhānī was collecting. In astonishment, Devarānī asked, "Where did you get this gold?" Jeṭhānī told her truthfully all that had happened the night before.

Seeing Jeṭhānī's fortune made Devarānī burn with jealousy. She resolved to save up all her broken rice that year. When Sakaṭh day came again, Devarānī prepared all kinds of sweets for her family and made some sweet balls from broken rice and bathuā greens to put under the plate on the altar. That night, Goddess Sakaṭh came to her house and said to her, "I am hungry." Devarānī lied, "Whatever I have is under the plate." Sakaṭh ate the sweets under the plate and then said, "I need to make bowel movement". Devarānī replied, "The whole house is clean; you can defecate wherever you wish." In the dark, it seemed to Devarānī that the goddess was excreting all over the house. She could hardly wait until morning to see all the gold she thought must be hers. When she woke up, however, see was dismayed to see her house full of excrement and all her riches gone.

Devarānī ran to Jeṭhānī's house and wept out the story. Jeṭhānī chided her, "You did all of this out of greed and performed the worship without faith; that is why you have been punished. I performed the worship with devotion and did not expect anything in return."[7] (BHAGWATI PANDEY—57—KANPUR CITY).

45. SACRIFICE OF A GOAT'S HEAD

There was a Brahman couple who was childless. They had tried every means of conceiving a child, but all had failed. Finally someone told them that they should ask Goddess Sakaṭh for help, so they went to her temple and promised that they would celebrate her worship with joy if they were blessed with a son.

A son was born after nine months, but the couple neglected to worship Sakaṭh, saying, "We are too busy right now." At the child's pasanī and muṇḍan ceremonies, they said, "We don't have enough money to worship Sakaṭh now." They made another excuse for not worshipping Sakaṭh on the occasion of the boy's janeū ceremony. At the time of the boy's marriage, many people told the Brahman that he should perform Sakaṭh's worship, but he said, "I will perform the worship after the wedding is over."

Goddess Sakaṭh became angry at last and decided to teach the couple a lesson. During the main wedding ceremony, she snatched the groom away from the *mañḍap* (marriage canopy) just as he began the seventh round of the fire. Everybody looked for him, but he couldn't be found anywhere, so the groom's party returned home sadly with the would-be bride.

Meanwhile, Goddess Sakaṭh hid the groom in a well near the house. Whenever his bride went to fetch water from the well, the groom held her rope and said, "You are my bride; you should free me. Tell your mother-in-law to worship Goddess Sakaṭh." Unfortunately, the poor girl could not understand what he said and thus one year passed. Finally, the girl told her mother-in-law, "Whenever I go to the well, someone down inside grabs my pot and says something to me." The next day the monther-in-law accompanied her to the well and discovered that it was her own son inside the well. She prayed to Goddess Sakaṭh for her son's freedom, but Sakaṭh told her, "You can have your son back only if you perform my worship on my appointed day."

The boy's mother waited for the day of Sakaṭh to come and then performed the worship lavishly; her son was then released from the well. When the boy came home, his relatives made him cut off a goat's head as a sacrificial offering. Thus the tradition of sacrificing a goat started.[8] (GEETA TIWARI—26—KANPUR CITY).

45a. VARIATION ON STORY NO. 45

Once a childless woman prayed to Mother Sakaṭh, "If I am blessed with a son, I will sacrifice a he-goat weighing 1¼ *paserī* (a unit of weight)." The goddess heard her prayer, and in due course the woman gave birth to a son. In her happiness, however, she forgot her promise. She performed the child's chaṭhi, muñḍan, pasanī, and janeū, but she neglected Mother Sakaṭh's worship.

In time, she arranged the boy's marriage. The boy knew that he would die as soon as he started the seventh round of the sacrificial fire, because his mother had not worshipped the goddess. When he arrived at the bride's home, he quietly asked the gardner's wife to arrange for him to talk to the bride. The gardener's wife showed him where the bride was playing with her friends, but as soon as she saw the groom, she started to run away. "Please stop and listen to me," he pleaded. Shyly, the girl returned and he told her, "During the ceremony, when we start on the seventh round of the fire, sit down and put my head in your lap. If I die, don't let anyone dispose of my body; keep it on a comfortable bed in my father's garden. Stay near my dead body during the day; climb a tree at night." "I will remember your words," promised the birde-to-be.

In the early hours of the morning, the first six rounds of the fire were completed without any trouble, but at the beginning of the seventh, the groom collapsed and the bride put his head on her lap. Soon he died. All the people present were frightened by this inauspicious event and wanted to prepare a funeral bier. The bride protested, "I will not let you take my husband's body away from me. Carry it to his father's garden and lay it on a fine bed." Thinking she had lost her mind from grief and shame, the girl's parents begged and pleaded with her. "What good will this do?" they reasoned, but the bride stood firm.

The groom's body was laid on a bed in his father's garden; the bride watched over it all day and then climbed a tree when the sun went down. That night Mother Sakaṭh came and moved the groom's pillow from his head to his feet; the groom arose immediately, and the goddess fed him, bathed him, and gave him fresh clothing. The bride observed all this from her perch in the tree, so the next day she too moved the pillow, to bring the groom back to life. From then on, the newlyweds ate together, talked, and enjoyed life during the daytime; at nightfall, the bride would put the pillow back under the groom's head and climb the tree.

Before long, Mother Sakaṭh noticed that someone else was caring for the groom during the day. To prevent this, she surrounded him with a brick wall. Still the bride managed to visit her husband every day. Eventually, she realized that she was pregnant. She was frightened that no one would believe her story. "I will be cast out by everyone!" she wept. "Don't worry;" her husband tried to calm her. "Go to my father's home and tell them everything. They will shelter you and care for you."

When Mother Sakaṭh learned that the bride was pregnant, she took the groom away with her. Now the bride found herself truly alone there, so she had no choice but to go to her in-laws' home. She told the story from beginning to end, and her mother-in-law gave her a place to live.

In due course, the girl gave birth to a son. In order to make her comfortable, her mother-in-law hired a *dhanukin* (a woman of the *dhānuk* caste) to care for her. Each night her husband appeared and asked her how she was faring. She always replied, "Your mother is very kind and treats me very well." One night the dhanukin overheard this conversation; she repeated it to the boy's mother in the morning. The mother wept, "Find out if there is any way I can get my son back." The next night the dhanukin pretended to be alseep, but when the bride's husband appeared, she called out, "Your mother wants to know if there is any way to bring you back." He told her, "My mother promised to offer a 1¼ paserī goat to Mother Sakaṭh if she begot a son, but she never once worshipped Sakaṭh after I was born. That is why I died on my wedding day. Now she must offer a 1¼ man[9] goat and invite all the gods and goddesses to a feast. Mother Sakaṭh will also come. As soon as my mother sees Sakaṭh, she should run and prostrate herself at Sakaṭh's feet."

The dhanukin told all this to the boy's mother, who hurried to arrange the feast. When the boy's wife prostrated before Mother Sakaṭh, the goddess blessed her (not realizing who she was), saying, "You shall have seven sons and your husband shall live as long as you do." The gods and goddesses finished eating and Mother Sakaṭh arose to go, calling the boy to her. The other gods and goddesses protested, "You cannot take him, for you have promised his wife seven sons and a happy married life." Realizing what had happened, Sakaṭh grabbed the boy and started to run, but the boy's mother fell at her feet, begging for forgiveness and promised to worship her regularly from then on.

May everyone's luck change, as hers did. (PHOOLMATI—81—SHEOLI).

45b. VARIATION ON STORY NO. 45

Once a widowed Jeṭhānī lived with her Devarānī. The family was well-off, but Jeṭhānī felt sad because she had no children and worried that the property and name of her late husband would be lost when she died. One day Jeṭhānī prayed to Sankaṭha *Maharānī*, "Oh, goddess, if you give me a son, I will host a feast in your honor."

By the grace of Shankar*ji*, a blister appeared on Jeṭhānī's hand. The blister grew and grew until one day it gave her a great deal of pain. Devarānī and other relatives gave her all kinds of medicines, but none of them worked. Finally the blister broke and a beautiful baby boy came out of it.[10] Jeṭhānī said, "I have been blessed with a son without a husband, so I myself cut the umbilical cord." There was great rejoicing in the family, but Jethānī became so busy in caring for the child that she forgot to worship Sankaṭha Maharānī. The boy's chaṭhī, barahoñ, muñḍan, pasanī, chedan, and janeū were performed lavishly, but Sakaṭh's worship was neglected completely.

When the boy was 11 years old, his marriage was arranged. During the marriage ceremony, he became ill. People asked Jethānī if she had forgotten to do any worship, but she said, "No." Shankar*ji* and Parvati heard all of this. The daughter-in-law came home but the boy's health deteriorated rapidly. One day the daughter-in-law was alone in a room; she heard a voice say, "Your husband belongs to one who didn't perform my worship." The daughter-in-law told this to her mother-in-law, who suddenly remembered her debt to Sankaṭha Maharānī. She performed the worship immediately. Her son soon regained his health, and they all lived happily together. (BUDDHAMATI—48—SHEOLI).

46. STEALING IS SINFUL IN THE MONTH OF MĀGH

Once there lived a poor man and his wife. When the time came for their daughter to go to her husband's home, the poor couple had nothing to present to her and the son-in-law. They also needed money so their son could bring his wife home to live with them. The poor woman pleaded with her husband, "Somehow you must bring ingredients for good food and presents to send with our daughter."

That night, the poor man went to a merchant's shop and hid himself in the warehouse. He couldn't bring himself to steal, however, and began to mutter, "*Til corāvañ to pāp, guḍ corāvañ to pāp, Māh kā mahīnā pāpai pāp*" (It would be sinful for me to steal sesame seeds. It would be sinful for me to steal guḍ. In the month of Māgh, it is sinful to steal anything).

The whole night passed. Early in the morning, the merchant's wife heard the poor man talking to himself in this manner. She told her husband, who went down to the warehouse and found the poor man in hiding. "Who are you?" demanded the merchant. "Please forgive me. I am a thief," moaned the poor man. "What kind of thief are you?" observed the merchant. "You haven't taken anything." "Oh," wept the poor man, "I must send my daughter to her in-laws' home and I also want to bring my daughter-in-law to my home, but I don't have any food in my house, nor any money to buy presents. I came to steal from you, but I couldn't do it because I remembered that this is the month of Māgh, when it is sinful to steal."

Hearing this, the merchant told the poor man gently, "Go home and prepare for your daughter's departure and your daughter-in-law's arrival." The merchant supplied him with a cart full of everything needed for the two events and the poor couple lived happily the rest of their lives. (BHAGWATI SHUKLA—54—VARANASI).

47. "ONE-NIGHT" SON

A man had just left home to travel abroad to find some work, when he overheard a snatch of conversation, "If someone is blessed with a son in one night (*ek ratiyā bālak*), the son will become a king." Upon hearing this, the man returned home and made love to his wife, without anyone noticing his presence. The woman became pregnant as a result, but when the pregnancy became obvious, her mother-in-law thought that she had committed adultery and told her to leave the house.

At their last meeting, the woman's husband had spit his betel saliva in one corner, left his sword, and sown some grain, telling his wife that he would know that she was chaste if these things remained fresh. The daughter-in-law showed all these signs to her mother-in-law, but she didn't believe her and proceeded to throw her out of the house. The unfortunate daughter-in-law went to a potter, who kindly gave her a room to live in. There she was soon blessed with a son.

After many years, her husband returned, bringing a cartload of riches with him. When he passed the potter's home, however, his cart got caught on a bush and no one could make it budge an inch. Inside the potter's house, the woman knew that her husband had returned. It was Mother Sakaṭh's fast day, and she was observing the fast. She worshipped the Ganesh Cauth and offered a whole betel nut in the worship, as a remover of evil. Her son observed this and took the betel nut to help move the cart.

In the meantime, the husband had promised half his wealth to whomever could move his cart. The son came and touched the cart with the blessed betel nut and, lo and behold, the cart instantly moved. The husband divided the riches into two parts, but as soon as he finished separating them, the two parts became one again. This happened many times, finally the man said, "Let us worry about this later," and hurried on to his home.

When he got home, he looked all over for his wife and finally asked his mother, "Everyone is here except my wife. Where is she?" His mother told him, "Your wife was unfaithful to you, so I made her leave." Hearing this, the husband went to his room and saw that his betel saliva was still fresh, the grain growing, and his sword shining. He told his mother, "The child is mine," and went to the potter's home to bring his wife and son back. (BHAGWATI SHUKLA—54—VARANASI).

47a. VARIATION ON STORY NO. 47

In this variation, the man leaves home on the day of Sakaṭh. He hears a bird in a *pīpal* tree say, "If anyone going abroad on the day of Sakaṭh goes back to his house that night and copulates with his wife, he will be blessed with a 'one-night son', who will be brave, beautiful, and intelligent." The man goes back and sleeps with his wife, who is then fearful of what will happen if she becomes pregnant. The man leaves his ring, handkerchief, sword, and betel saliva in one corner, as tokens of his presence. He urinates in another spot and plants barley there, to prevent his mother from mistreating his wife. Nevertheless, the woman's mother-in-law and sister-in-law throw her out of the house.

She hides in the manger of a potter's kiln, hoping to die when the potter lights the fire. Instead, she gives birth to twins in the midst of the pottery firing. She tells her story to the astonished potter and his wife, who take pity on her and give her a room in their house.

Her husband returns after twelve years, with a money-laden cart that gets caught on a small plant. Priests and astrologers inform him that the cart can be freed only by one who is 'one-night of Sakaṭh born." People remember that the woman who lives with the potters had twins born on the night of Sakaṭh, so they are sent for. The woman tells her sons not to touch the cart unless the man promises to give them half the load. The man finally agrees, but is unable to keep the riches divided. When the boys touch the cart, however, the load divides of its own accord and the cart is freed.

The boys take their share home to the potter's house and the man returns to his home, only to discover his wife missing. He shows the ring and other tokens to his mother and sister, who then feel ashamed for their unkindness. The woman and her sons are brought home with great rejoicing, and everyone lives happily together from then on. (PHOOLMATI—81—SHEOLI).

48. THE FEAST OF SANKAṬHA

There was an old woman whose son had lived abroad for 12 years. One day when she went to fetch water from the well, she saw some women offering a feast to the Goddess Sañkaṭhā. She asked the women, "Why do you perform the feast to Sañkaṭhā?" They replied, "If anyone wants a desire fulfilled, he or she can pray to goddess Sañkaṭhā and promise her a feast."

The old woman prayed fervently, "If my son comes back, I will host a feast for Sañkaṭhā." Her son returned a few days later, and the old woman joyously prepared the feast of Sañkaṭhā. (PUSHPA-LATA—41—SHEOLI).

49. THE MAGIC COOKING POT

Once Ganesh*ji* was roaming the countryside disguised as a child, carrying a little rice and milk with him and asking everyone to make khīr for him. Wherever he went people refused, telling him, "Chew the rice and drink the milk. How can one make khīr out of such a small amount of rice and milk?" Ganesh*ji*, however, kept asking.

Finally he approached a *gaḍariyā* (a shepherd) woman who was busy taking care of her cows and goats. She said, "Come dear child. If nobody else will make khīr for you, I will do it." She put a small pot on the fire, but Ganesh*ji* said, "No, no, mother, put a *baṭuā* (a cooking pot) on the fire." The woman felt a little annoyed, but decided to humor the child and thus put her biggest pot on the fire.

The child disappeared, but the woman began to prepare the khīr. As soon as the fire touched the baṭuā, it became full with khīr, so she poured it into a bucket. The baṭuā was still full, however, so she filled another pot, and another, and another, until all her pots were full. Her daughter-in-law couldn't understand what she was doing. "She won't let me eat, but keeps finding more work for me to do. I'm going to eat anyway. There is plenty of khīr."

Her mother-in-law waited for the child to come. The child returned just before sunset. "Where did you go?" the woman chided. "I have been waiting for you all day. See how much khīr came out of the baṭuā? My daughter-in-law and I are both hungry, but you eat first." Then the all-knowing child informed her, "Mother, your daughter-in-law has already eaten the khīr." Ganesh*ji* revealed his true form to the woman and blessed her.[11] (BUDDHAMATI—48—SHEOLI).

50. RIVER SISTERS

Ganga-ceri and Jamuna-ceri were sisters. One day when they were walking in the fields, a sesame seed stuck to the foot of Jamuna-ceri. Ganga-ceri said, "It is sinful to take sesame seeds in the month of Māgh. You must serve the farmer for twelve years. Then when he goes to take a bath in the Ganga, send two grains of barley with him. If I accept those grains, you will know that your sin has been atoned for."

Jamuna-ceri then sat in the field and waited until the farmer came. "Let me serve you, in payment for the sesame seed which stuck to my foot. The only things I will not do are make your bed or attend to your son's call of nature," she stipulated. The farmer agreed to these two conditions and Jamuna-ceri served him faithfully for twelve years. When the farmer and his family were leaving for a Ganga bath festival, Jamuna-ceri gave two grains of barley to the farmer's wife, asking her to offer them to the Ganga in her name.

The farmer's wife finished her bath, but forgot to offer the grains of barley. Immediately, the water started to rise. Then the farmer's wife remembered the barley grains, put them in her hands, and prayed, "My servant said to offer you these grains only if you received them in your hands." Mother Ganga then rose up and took the two grains of barley in her hands. The farmer's wife felt very sad and said to Mother Ganga, "I have worshipped you faithfully for years, but you have never revealed yourself to me. Why do you receive this small offering from my servant with such respect?" Mother Ganga replied, "Your servant is my sister. She served your family for twelve years in atonement for a sin. Return on your bare feet and serve Jamuna-ceri, and your services will be rewarded accordingly." (BETI DEVI—85—SHEOLI).

51. THE TRUE MOTHER'S TEST

There was a king who had a kiln which was fired every day. However, to fire the kiln, the king had to sacrifice a male child every day. He made a rule in his kingdom that every household would send a son according to a specific order. In his kingdom lived an old woman who had a son. On the day of Sakaṭh, other members of the community decided, "Today is Sakaṭh, so we should not send our sons; instead, let the old woman's son be sent." Accordingly, they told the old woman, "Today is your turn." The old woman immediately made preparations for the worship of Sakaṭh. After feeding her son, she told him, "Carry this wooden board on which I have drawn and worshipped the figures of Sakaṭh; clutch it to your stomach when you are put into the kiln, and keep reciting, 'True Sakaṭh, true Sakaṭh.' " Her son went obediently to the king and was put into the kiln. Throughout the night, the old woman meditated upon Mother Sakaṭh. In the morning the king saw his whole kiln turned into gold, with the old woman's son inside, reciting "True Sakaṭh, true Sakaṭh." The king sent out a drummer to announce to the whole kingdom, "Whoever sent this child should collect the gold." Everybody ran to claim, "He is my son!" The old woman dragged herself there as well, to claim her rightful due, but everyone rejected her plea, saying, "The boy is mine!" Then the king said, "All of you women must line up; whoever's milk goes into the child's mouth is the true mother of the child." All the women present formed a line and milk from the old woman's breasts gushed into the mouth of the child child. Thus the old woman was rewarded with the gold and lived happily ever after. (MAHADEVI--70—KANPUR CITY).

NOTES

1. The informant used the term "Sañkaṭhā" here to refer to Goddess Sakaṭh, although two distinct celebrations are inferred: (1) the festival of Sakaṭh, which is observed once a year, and (2) Sañkaṭhā ki Sohāgileñ, the feasting of married women after a desired wish has been granted. A woman makes a promise to Mother Sañkaṭhā to feed a certain number of married women upon fulfillment of her wish. In Story No. 42, Sañkaṭhā is used to designate the feast of Sañkathā. In story No. 48, "The Feast of Sañkaṭhā" describes the actual feeding of women. The story does not belong to the festival of Sakaṭh, but the informant nevertheless maintained that there was nothing wrong in telling the story of Sañkaṭhā during Sakaṭh.
2. When questioned, the informant clarified: "Gengata is an animal, but I don't know what kind."
3. See Gupte 1919:54; Lall 1933:172; and Dimmitt 1978:179.
4. This informant said this was a story for Ganesh Cauth. See Michael 1983: 91–116.
5. Goddess Sakaṭh is supposed to be seven sisters in one body.
6. See Tripathi 1977:475.
7. See Tripathi 1977:470; "The Katha of Ganeshcauth" in Wadley 1978:314-315. Similar stories were recorded from Bhagwati Shukla—54—Varanasi; Beti Devi—85—Sheoli and Mahadevi—70—Kanpur city.
8. See "The Story of Dasarani Vrat" in Sita 1970:128.
9. After the story was told, I questioned the informant about the 1¼ *man* goat. She answered that since no goat weights 1¼ *man*, she made a goat figure out of 1¼ *man* of black sesame seeds.
10. A legend, similar to this story, makes Kabir "the son of a Brahman widow born miraculously from the palm of her hand, as the result of prayer of the ascetic Ramanand, . . . " (Shah 1977: 3).
11. See Satyendra 1962:31 and Sita 1970:104.

Plate 13. Sakaṭh

A drawing on a wooden board, made with ghī, depicting five human images, called *Sakaṭh ke putale* (Sakaṭh's figures). The five lumps of mud represent Gauri. (Chaya Tiwari—22—Kanpur city).

Plate 14. Sakaṭh

Preparation for the worship of Sakaṭh. Seen are the wooden board with five images drawn in ghī, two plates full of food offerings (pūrīs, sweet balls made from different parched grains, sweet potatoes, bananas, and a goat made from black sesame seeds and gud syrup), and a metal pot filled with water and covered with a saucer containing rice which cushions a ghī-lamp. In front of the wooden board, a flower design is being made with flour.

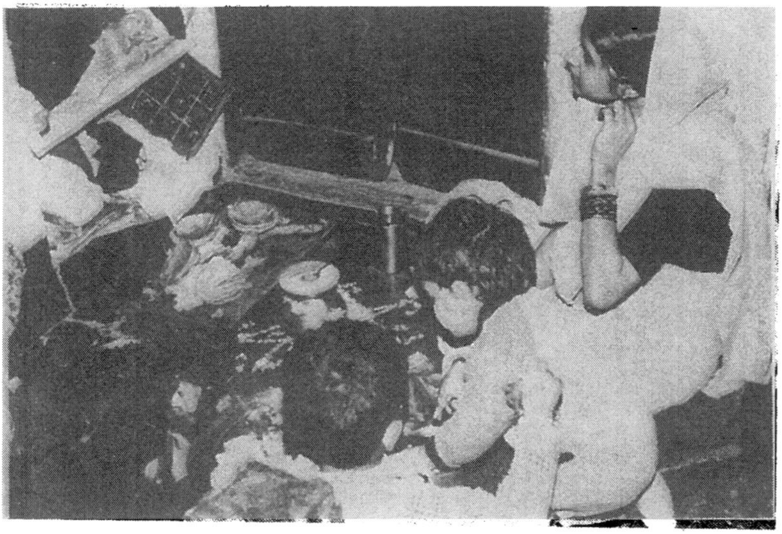

Plate 15. Worship of Sakaṭh

With all preparations ready, the head woman of the household begins the worship. She places the water-pot on the center of the flower design, offers food to the Sakaṭh images drawn on the wooden board, burns incense and the ghī-lamp, and tells stories. At the end of the worship, the boys of the household "slaughter" the sesame seed goat while bleating enthusiastically. Everybody present touches the feet of the Sakaṭh images and receives prasad.

XIV. ŚĪTALĀ ASṬAMĪ

Śītalā Asṭamī is observed on the eighth day of the dark half of Cait. All food is prepared the previous evening as no fires or cooking are allowed on this day. Women fast in honor of Mother Śītalā in order to protect their families from smallpox and other illnesses. Śītalā is greatly dreaded and widely worshipped. She is glorified with many names: "Mata, mother; Jagrani, Queen of the World; Maha Mai, Great Mother; Jagadamba, Mother of the earth; Kalejewali, She of the Liver; Tamdi, She that Loves the Cool; and Phapholewali, She of the Vesicle" (Briggs 1920:137). The previously prepared food is eaten by family members who are not observing the fast, thus this festival is often called *Baseurā* (leftover) *Asṭmī* also (see Lewis 1965:200).

Late in the morning, groups of women make the circuit of the local goddesses' shrines, singing songs in praise of Śītalā. In most cases, shrines consist of a few fetish stones placed under a *nīm* tree. Each village I visited had its own names of local goddesses. In Sheoli, for example, there were shrines dedicated to Goddesses Mal Sila, Pantha Bhavani, Maha Maiya, Isvari Maiya, and Phulamati Maiya.

52. SEVEN CLEVER PRINCESSES

There once lived a royal couple who didn't have any children. One day a fakīr came and told the king that he would become poor if he had any daughters. The king therefore told his queen to kill any daughters who might be born to them.

In time, the queen became pregnant. When she gave birth, she was dismayed to see that the child was a girl. The daughter was so beautiful, however, that her mother couldn't bear to kill her, so she hid the child in a *koṭhailā* (a large vessel for storing grain). As time passed, the queen gave birth to seven daughters and hid them all in the kothailā. Every time the king went out hunting, the girls came out to play; just before he returned, they all ran quickly to their hiding place.

As the fakīr had predicted, the king slowly became poor. He complained to his wife, "I am working very hard, but I get poorer every day." Still the queen kept the secret of his seven living daughters from him.

One day, when the king was out hunting and his daughters came out to play, one of the girls lost her ankle-bracelets in the garden. Later that day, the king went for a stroll in the garden and tripped on the ankle-bracelets. Immediately he questioned the queen, "Where did these come from? There are no children in the palace." The queen confessed that she had disobeyed him and had not killed their daughters after all. She begged his forgiveness and the king said, "Ah well, whatever has happened has happened. Make *khīr* (rice pudding) for our evening meal."

The queen decided to make the khīr after girls had gone to sleep. The daughters were clever, however, and each of them hid some of the kitchen utensils. When the queen got up to make the khīr, she couldn't find the wok. The youngest daughter whispered to her, "I will get the *kaḍhāī* (a cooking pot similar to the Chinese wok) for you." The queen replied, "Take care not to wake your sisters." One by one, the queen discovered that all of the utensils she needed were missing, and one by one, six of the girls got up. The eldest daughter was the cleverest, however, and stayed in her bed until the khīr was made. Then, when her mother wasn't looking, she slipped a brick into it to make the pot appear full, and the girls ate most of the khīr themselves.

When the queen was serving the khīr to the king, the brick fell onto his plate. Seeing this, the king berated her, "I told you to kill all daughters born to us, but you did not listen. Now we are truly poor." The queen wept, "I cannot kill them, not even now."

The next morning, the king asked his daughters to come with him to gather wild fruits in the forest. The queen put some food in bags for each of the six younger daughters; by the time she got to the seventh bag, there was no more food left, so she filled it with ashes[1] for the eldest daughter to eat.

After taking his daughters deep into the forest, the king shook a *ber* tree so that the daughters could eat the fruit. He hung his turban and a gong on the tree, saying, "When the gong rings and the turban flutters, you will know that your father is calling you and it is time for you to come home." Then he abandoned his daughters in the forest.

After a while, the wind began to blow, which made the gong ring and turban flutter. "It is time for us to go home," the younger daughters said. "No," said the eldest. "Our father left us here because he knew we would get lost in the forest. Let us forget about going home; we will eat whatever our mother has given us instead."

Each of the daughters began to eat what was in her bag. When the eldest opened her bag, she found only ashes, but she said nothing and began to eat. Soon the other sisters noticed, however, and gathered around her, saying, "Come, let us eat together and share everything with one another."

After a while, the eldest daughter said, "We should go to Brahma and ask why we have been left alone here." Together they went to Brahma and challenged him, "If you have given birth to us, you should also make us useful." Brahma told them, "You will become the Goddess Śītalā.[2] Go into the town and ask the potter to make mud horses for you."

The girls did as Brahma advised; soon the potter gave them seven mud horses. Then the eldest daughter declared, "If I am truly Śītạlā, let these horses become real." The mud horses came to life immediately and the girls mounted them gleefully. "Where shall we go first?" asked the youngest. "We should go to the palace," said the eldest, and the seven sisters galloped away.

They reined up in front of the royal palace and the eldest daughter told the children who were playing outside, "Go tell the king that his mother's sisters have come." When the children gave the king this message, he asked, "How have they come?" "Riding on mud horses," replied the children. Immediately the king ordered his guards to chain his daughters heavily and throw them in prison. As soon as the orders were carried out, however, everyone in the royal family broke out with smallpox, and many other things began to go wrong. Realizing his error, the king released his daughters.

Upon leaving the palace, the seven sisters went to the house of a Bhat whose son was suffering from smallpox. The Bhat's wife was on her way to the well to fetch water for her son when the seven sisters rode up and requested, "Please give some water to our horses." The woman broke her water jar and used the broken pieces to offer water to the seven horses. At home, her feverish child cried piteously for water. Her mother-in-law ran out to ask why she was taking so long. "I am serving the goddesses," replied the woman, and her son was immediately cured.

The Bhat's family celebrated the miracle of the child's recovery with great rejoicing, while everyone at the king's palace was suffering. The Bhat thought to himself, "If the king is happy, all his people are happy, too. But if the king is sad, all his subjects are sad." The Bhat therefore asked the seven sisters to give a son to the king After much pleading, he finally convinced the seven sisters, who told him, "The king and queen can be blessed with a son only if they serve us faithfully for twelve years."

The Bhat went and told this to the king and queen, who then worked as laborers for twelve years and were finally blessed with a beautiful son.[3] (PUSHPALATA—41—SHEOLI).

52a. VARIATION ON STORY NO. 52

Once there was a king who had seven daughters and was very poor. One day the king said to his queen, "I want to eat khīr today." His queen complained, "How can I make khīr? Our daughters will eat it all." The king begged his wife, until finally she said, "All right, I will make it after our daughters go to sleep."

The daughters overheard this conversation, however, so before going to sleep, each daughter hid one of the kitchen utensils. When the queen got up to make the khīr, she couldn't find any of the pots, cups, bowls, or spoons she needed. One daughter got up and said, "I know where your big pot is." "Bring it to me," said her mother, "but take care that you don't wake your sisters." One by one, however, each of the daughters awoke and got up to give her mother a utensil.

When the khīr was made, the queen thought, "I'll have to give some of it to my daughters, but I will give them the thin khīr from the top and save the thick khīr on the bottom for my husband." The daughters were so clever, however, that they put a brick in the pot. Their mother served them the khīr from the top, but when she went to serve the king, there was nothing left but the brick.

The queen was so angry at her daughters for tricking her that she told the king to take them to the forest and abandon them. The king tried to dissuade the queen, but she insisted. Early the next morning, the queen gave each of the seven daughters a lunch sack and the king took them into the forest. He hung a bell and his turban on a tree and told them, "When the bell rings and the turban flutters, you will know that your father has come back." Then the king left his seven daughters in the forest and returned to the palace.

For a while the girls enjoyed gathering wild fruits and eating them. In the meantime, the wind made the bell ring and the turban flutter, so they kept thinking that their father was returning. Nobody came, however, and slowly they realized that they had been abandoned. Eventually they found a well, where they bathed and then sat down to eat whatever their mother had given them. The first six daughters each had something good to eat (such as pūrī, gojhiyā, *gulguḷā* or *āsai*), but the youngest daughter found only ashes in her sack. After she had eaten two mouthfuls of ashes, her sisters noticed what she was eating and stopped her, saying, "We will share what we have with one another."

After they had eaten, the sisters played around the well and made horses out of the mud. Climbing on their horses' backs, they declared, "If we are honest and true, these mud-horses should walk for us." Immediately their horses began to prance about. "Let us go see Brahma," the sisters decided. When they found Brahma, they demanded, "If you have given birth to us, you should also give us good deeds to perform." Brahma promised them, "In Kaliyug, you will become Śītalā." "How will we know that?" asked the seven sisters. Brahma then replied, "If you cut your left little fingers and sprinkle some blood onto something, it will be affected with a severe fever, followed by smallpox, and marks like split chickpeas will be left on it."

The sisters then left Brahma and found a big nīm tree, which they sprinkled with blood from their left little fingers. The tree immediately began to suffer from severe fever and smallpox; marks as big as split chickpeas were left all over the tree. The tree thought, "I am a big tree, yet I have suffered greatly from them. How could a person survive this affliction?" He begged the sisters, "Give only one-fourth strength of this to human beings." The sisters promised, and then went on to try their power on a stone and a cow.

After that, the sisters debated, "Where shall we go to try our power over human beings, to the king's palace or to the Bhat's house?" They decided to go to the king's palace first. When they arrived there, the king was informed, "Your mother's sisters have come." Suspiciously, the king asked the messenger, "How have they come?" The messenger described them, "Riding on mud horses, with noses sniveling and saliva dribbling." The king then commanded his guards, "Sprinkle hot oil on them and tie them to iron rods." This was done, but the seven sisters soon escaped.

Upon leaving the palace, the sisters went to the Bhat's house, where his son was suffering from smallpox. When they arrived the Bhat's wife was bathing Goddess Śītalā in her temple. As she poured water from her earthen pot onto the Goddess, some of it splashed onto the seven sisters. They blessed her, saying, "As you have cooled us today, you and your family shall also enjoy the cool nature of Śītalā."

Meanwhile, the woman's son was asking for water at home. Her mother-in-law scolded her when she returned, saying, "What took you so long to fetch the water, when your son is suffering so?" The Bhat's wife replied, "I was serving the Goddess," and her son recovered immediately. In happiness, musicians were invited to play and everyone rejoiced.

At the king's palace, however, people began dying of smallpox. When the king heard the music at the Bhat's house, he asked, "Where is that music coming from?" Someone told him, "The Bhat is rejoicing, because the Goddess is pleased with him." Angrily, the king ordered the Bhat thrown in prison.

The Bhat's wife went to the Goddess' temple, weeping, "I am in terrible trouble now, for my husband has been imprisoned by the king." "Don't worry," the Goddess consoled her. "Go home and your husband will be freed." Miraculously, the Bhat's handcuffs opened of their own accord and clamped onto the king's hands. The Bhat returned to his home, where the music started up again. The handcuffed king asked again, "Where is that music coming from?" He was told, "The Bhat is rejoicing, for the Goddess has blessed him again."

Then the king ordered the Bhat brought before him again. Humbly, the king pleaded, "Go to the Goddess and tell her, 'If the king is happy, the people are happy.' " The Bhat therefore went to the Goddess and asked her to release the king from his handcuffs and relieve the sufferings of his household. The Goddess refused at first, but finally yielded, saying, "Tell the king that he and his queen must work as laborers. She must fill baskets with mud and he must carry them. Only then will they be free of my anger." The king and queen performed this penance and finally were pardoned by the Goddess. (BHAGWATI SHUKLA—54—VARANASI).

53. THE CONTEST BETWEEN DEVI AND HANUMAN

One day Hanuman and Devi started fighting over their relative statuses. Hanuman said, "I am the greatest!" Devi contradicted him, "No, I am greater than you!" In order to settle the dispute, Devi challenged Hanuman, "Whoever can bring presents from the village shall be considered greater."

Hanuman accepted the challenge and went to the village. It was the day of Śītalā Aṣṭamī, however, and everywhere Hanuman went, people told him, "We cannot give you anything without worshipping Śītalā first." Hanuman therefore came back empty-handed.

Devi then picked up her basket and went to the village. Everywhere she went, women rushed to give her offerings. Devi thus came back with her basket full. "Now who do you think is the greater?" she asked Hanuman. Hanuman acknowledged his defeat and said, "*Jahāñ tumhār jāp, tahāñ hamār thāp* (Wherever people worship you, my protection will be there, too).[4] (PUSHPALATA—41—SHEOLI).

54. THE JEALOUS QUEENS

There once lived a king who had six queens but remained childless. He married a seventh time and shortly thereafter his seventh queen became pregnant. The other six queens were terribly jealous and plotted to take the child away from her. The seventh queen was so naive that she asked the other queens, "What happens at the time of childbirth?" "Don't worry," they said, "We will just blindfold you and you will have a son." When the seventh queen mentioned this to the king, he cautioned her, "Don't ask the other queens any more questions. Ring this bell when the time comes, and I will come to help you deliver the child."

The pregnant queen thus stopped asking the other queens questions. Before long, they approached her, "Don't you need our help? Do you think you know everything about childbirth?" The innocent queen told them exactly what the king had told her. "Oh!" they laughed at her, "Do you really think he will come? Why don't you try to summon him now?" The seventh queen foolishly took their bait and ran to ring the bell. The king came immediately, but when he realized he was being tested, he became very angry. "When you ring the bell again, I will not come!" he warned her.

Eventually the queen began to feel labor pains. She rang the bell, but the king did not come to help. Instead, the other six queens quickly blindfolded her. A son was born, but the queens whisked him away and put stones in his place. When the king asked about his child, the six queens told him, "Your seventh queen has given birth to stones." Angrily, the king banished the seventh queen from the city, telling her, "You can keep the birds away from the city."

Meanwhile, the other queens hid the newborn child in a potter's kiln. When the potter came, he was unable to extinguish the fire under the kiln. In desperation, he offered half his wealth to anyone who could put out the fire. Everyone in the city tried, including the king and his six queens, but all failed. Finally the unfortunate seventh queen was summoned; as soon as she came near the kiln, milk flowed from her breasts and quenched the fire. The potter opened the kiln and found all his pots turned to gold and Mother Asai sitting there with a beautiful baby boy on her lap. Everyone exclaimed, "Who are you? Why are you sitting here?" The Goddess replied, "I am Mother Asai and I am caring for the child of the seventh queen of this kingdom, because she has worshipped me faithfully since her childhood. The other six queens blindfolded her during her son's birth and threw him into this potter's kiln."

Hearing this, the king begged for his son, but Mother Asai stipulated, "Throw your six queens alive into a grave, bring a palanquin for your seventh queen, and then you may have your son." The six wicked queens were therefore buried alive, the king came back to the kiln riding an elephant, and a palanquin was brought for the seventh queen and her son. The royal family returned to the palace and lived happily ever after.[5] (BHAGWATI SHUKLA—54—VARANASI).

55. A VAIN QUEEN LEARNS THE VALUE OF PIETY

There once lived a king who was poor, but very pious. Because of the good life he led, his wife was able to draw water from a deep well, using only a thread and an unbaked earthen pot, and she was able to suspend her *sari* in the sky to dry.

One day while the queen was drawing water, she overheard two birds talking in a nearby tree. "What kind of queen is she that she does not wear beautiful earrings and other jewelry?" they wondered. Hearing this, the queen returned to the palace and went straight to bed.

Finding his wife so depressed, the king asked, "What is wrong, dear wife?" "I want some jewelry," wept the queen. "I am a poor king and cannot afford it," reasoned the king, but the queen insisted. Finally the king ordered all of his subjects to bring a certain amount of money to him; with the money collected, he bought some jewels for his queen.

The next day when the queen went to the well, her thread broke, the earthen pot broke, and her sari fell down from the sky. Sadly, she returned home and went to bed again. "What is wrong now?" asked the confused king. "Return the money you asked from your subjects," wept the queen, "and add one-fourth more to it. Piety is better than wealth."

The king sold the jewels and returned the money to the people with interest. The following day the queen drew water from the well with her thread and unbaked earthen pot and hung her sari in the sky to dry.[6] (BHAGWATI SHUKLA—54—VARANASI).

NOTES

1. Ashes symbolize the Goddess Śītalā.
2. "[Sītalā] is one of seven sisters who are supposed to cause pustular diseases. One is Masani, who plagues people with boils. Agawani is the fever-goddess, who heats the body. Sītalā's elder sister, Chamariya, is the disease in its worst form. Her younger sister, Phulmati, represents the mild form of smallpox. The other sisters are Basanti and Lamhariya" (Briggs 1920:137–38). See also Crooke 1896:1.128.
3. See Pandey 1967:8 and "The Seven Sisters" in Mohanti 1975:109.
4. See Pandey 1967:7. Another informant, Bhagwati Shukla—54—Varanasi, told a similar story, wherein the challenge is to bring back some fire from the village. Villagers tell Hanuman, "Today is *Besaurā*, so we don't have any fire." Devi goes disguised as a gardener's wife and is given puris, sweets, and flowers by everyone, thus winning the contest.
5. See "The Nine Score and One Babies," "The Brave Child," and "The Tale of Lalpila" in Elwin 1944:202–12; "The Seven Sisters" in Mohanti 1975:109; Pandey 1967:11; "Lal" in Parmar 1975:190; Tripathi 1977:474; and "The Story of Seven Brothers and a Sister" in Majumdar 1971:1.
6. See Pandey 1967:17.

GLOSSARY

Agahan: the ninth month of the Hindu year
ahīr: the caste which herds cows and buffalo and sells milk; a member of this caste
āhuti: offering oblations to the fire during worship
aipan: a thin paste made from pounded rice and water
amāvasyā: the last day of the dark half of the month
Annakūṭ: a festival to honor Goddess Annakūṭ
arahar: a kind of lentil, *citisus cajan*
ārati: a ritual performed during the worship of gods and goddesses, when a lighted lamp or burning camphor is waved circularly in front of the idol
araval: *ayurbal* (the continuation of life) has become *araval*, by a village etymology; a roll of cotton (*pūnī*) about 12″ long, which is squeezed and dabbed with *rocanā* at 1″ intervals
Asāḍh: the fourth month of the Hindu year
āsai: deep-fried oval pieces of sweet wheat dough
Ashok Asṭamī: see *Avaī Āṭhai*
asṭamī: the eighth day in either half of the month
Avaī Āṭhai: a fast observed by married women on the eighth day of the dark half of *Kārtik* (see Chapter VII)
baḍavā: one whose tail is cut
badī: the dark half of the month
Baḍī Ekādasī: a worship to celebrate the awakening of the gods (see Chapter XII)
Bahurā Cauth: a fast observed by mothers on the fourth day in the dark half of the month of *Bhādau*, to protect their sons (see Chapter V)
Baisākh: the second month of the Hindu year
bājarā: millet
bañjārā: a wandering grain-dealer, a nomad community
baragad: a banyan tree
Baragadāhī: a festival observed by married women, on the last day of the dark half of *Jeṭh*, for the prosperity and long lives of their husbands (see Chapter II)
barahoṅ: the ceremony performed on the twelfth day after a child's birth
bārī: a caste which prepares and sells items made of leaves (bowls, plates, etc.)
baseurā: food prepared one day in advance; leftover
Baseurā Asṭamī: see *Śītalā Asṭamī*
bathuā: a green leafy vegetable (*chenopodium album*)
baṭuā: a metal cooking pot
ber: a tropical berry
berausī: a clay bowl used to burn cowdung cakes or soft coal
besaurā: see *baseurā*
bhābhī: elder brother's wife
Bhādau: the sixth month of the Hindu year

Bhaiyā Dūj: a festival for brothers and sisters, performed on the second day of the bright half of *Kārtik* (see Chapter X)
bhaṭakaṭaiyā: a prickly shrub
bhaujāī: elder brother's wife
bhaujī: elder brother's wife
buā: father's sister
Cait: the first month of the Hindu year
canā: small brown chickpeas
cāturmās: the four months when the gods sleep; the four months of the rainy season
caturthī: the fourth day in either half of the month
caurāī: a green vegetable (*amaranthus polygamus*)
cāval: rice
chaṭhī: the ceremony performed on the sixth day after a child's birth
chedan: the ceremony of piercing a child's ears
chikuliyā: a kind of tree
Ciraiyā Gaur: a ritual observed by married women on the first day of the bright half of *Kārtik*, to assure their husband's love (see Chapter VIII)
ciuḍā: flattened rice
cukaḍiyā: a small clay pot
darśan: auspicious sight
devar: husband's younger brother
devarānī: husband's younger brother's wife
dhānuk: a caste whose traditional occupation is rice-threshing; a member of this caste
dhanukin: a woman of the *dhānuk* caste; see *dhānuk*
dharm-kī-bahan: the custom of a girl or woman tying a thread on the wrist of a boy or man, to make him her "brother"
dhobin: a washerwoman
Dīpāvalī: the festival of lights
dupaṭṭā: scarf
durkaiyāṅ: the ritual of worshipping seven women in one's home and feeding them parched chickpeas and rice
dūrvā: a kind of grass used in rituals (*agrostis linearis*)
gaḍariyā: a caste which herds animals; a member of this caste
gaunā: the ceremony performed before taking a bride to her husband's home for the first time after marriage, at the onset of puberty
gehūṅ: wheat
ghanaucī: a raised platform for storing pots filled with water
ghī: clarified butter, used in rituals and special food preparations
ghugharī: boiled wheat and chickpeas eaten during the festival of *Nāg Pañcamī*
Gobardhan: a festival for the worship of Mount Gobardhan (see Chapter IX)
gojhiyā: a deep-fried turnover, filled with cream of wheat or *khoyā* and nuts
guḍ: crude brown sugar
guḍiyā: doll
Guḍiyā-kā-melā: the festival of dolls (see Chapter IV)
gulgulā: deep-fried sweet balls made with wheat dough and sugar
gurdhaniyā: parched wheat mixed with raw sugar and made into balls

Harachaṭh: a fast observed by women on the sixth day of the dark half of *Bhādau* for the well-being of their sons (see Chapter VI)
harahaiyā: a wild cow
Haritālikā: see *Tīj*
Jagannāth: a fast observed on Monday in the bright half of *Cait* (see Chapter I)
Jadgīsh Swāmī: see *Jagannāth*
jālī-chūlī: a thorny berry bush
Jam-Jaminā: Lord Yam and his wife
janeū: the sacred thread worn by men of the twice-born castes; the sacred thread ceremony
Jeṭh: the third month of the Hindu year; husband's elder brother
jeṭhānī: husband's elder brother's wife
jharaberī: a berry bush
jhula ke git: swinging song
jotā-ann: plough-produced food
jvār: a kind of millet
kaḍhāī: a cooking pot similar to the Chinese wok
kaḍhī: a soup made with buttermilk or thinned yogurt, chickpea flour, and spices
kahānī: (pl. *kahāniyāñ*) story
kajalī (kajarī): a type of song sung during the rainy season
kajarauṭī: a container for *kājal* (a mixture of lampblack and other ingredients)
kālā namak: black rock salt
kapilā: a domestic cow
karma: deeds or work
Kārtik: the eighth month of the Hindu year
karvā: an earthen pot with a spout
Karvā Cauth: a festival observed by married women on the fourth day of the bright half of *Kārtik* (see Chapter XI)
kasār: wheat meal fried in ghi and mixed with sugar
kathā: (pl. *kathāyeñ*) story
khalihān: threshing area
khicaḍī: a dish prepared with rice and lentils
khīr: a sweet dish, made of rice cooked in milk
khoyā: milk which has been reduced to a solid by boiling
kissā: a secular story
koḍvār: the practice of increasing food preparations for a celebration in thanks for good fortune in the family (*e.g.*, marriage or birth of a son) during the preceding year; the extra food is distributed among relatives and neighbors
koṭhailā: a large earthen vessel for storing grain
krishna paksh: the dark half of the lunar month
kuṭkuṭī: a bird
kūṭū: a plant whose seeds are ground into flour
Kvār: the seventh month of the Hindu year
laḍḍū: sweet balls
lahañgā: skirt
lapasī: a thin pudding made by frying flour in *ghī* and adding water and sugar
maciyā: a sitting stool
Māgh: the eleventh month of the Hindu year
Mahārānī: great queen

mahāvar: a red dye which women use to paint their feet on happy occasions
mahuā: the tree *bassia latifolia*; fruit of the mahua tree
makāī: corn
man: a unit of weight, equivalent to forty seers
mañdap: marriage canopy; a plank of mango-wood, which is set in the ground at the place where marriage ceremony is to be held
maṭar: peas
misrī: sugar candy
moksh: liberation from the cycle of rebirth
muñḍan: the ceremony of shaving a child's hair
murgī: hen
Nāglok: the abode of snakes
Nāg Pañcamī: a festival to honor snakes, performed on the fifth day of the bright half of *Sāvan* (see Chapter IV)
nanad: husband's sister
nārī: a tropical green vegetable; a woman
nenū: butter
nīm: the margosa tree
nirjalā: total abstinence from eating and drinking
paisā: pice
paksh: fortnightly halves of the month
pakauḍī: chopped vegetables mixed with chickpea flour batter and deep-fried
palās: the tree *butea frondosa*
parachan: a ceremony, performed at the time of marriage, in which a lamp is moved round the head of the bridegroom and bride to drive away evil spirits
pasaī-ke-cāval: wild rice
pasanī: the ceremony of feeding a child its first solid food
paserī: a weight of five seers
pāṭā: a flat wooden board used for sitting
Phāgun: the twelfth month of the Hindu year
phaldān: the ceremony in which a bride's relatives go to the groom's house with presents, part of the dowry, and a paper designating the times for the marriage ceremonies
pharā: deep-fried flat circular cakes made from chickpea flour
phulaurī: deep-fried balls made from chickpea flour and soaked in *kaḍhī*
pinnī: rice flour mixed with sugar and water and made into balls
pīpal: a tree sacred to Hindus
prasād: food offered to a deity and then distributed to those present; that which is given out of divine favor
puā: a sweet deep-fried flat bread
pūrī: a deep-fried flat bread
purnimāvasyā: the last day of the bright half of the month
Pūs: the tenth month of the Hindu year
rocanā: see *tilak*
roṭī: a flat, unleavened bread partly cooked over a round plate of iron and partly over direct flames
Sakaṭh: a fast observed by married women on the fourth day of the dark half of *Māgh* (see Chapter XIV)

sañyāsī: an ascetic
sasur: wife's or husband's father
Sāvan: the fifth month of the Hindu year; a song type
Sāvitrī Pūjā: see *Baragadāhī*
sendur: red powder traditionally worn in the part of the hair by married women
seer: a weight equal to 2.057 pounds
siṅghāḍā: the thorny fruit of the water-plant *trapanataus*
sīṅk: wicker
Śītalā Aṣṭamī: a fast observed on the eighth day of the dark half of *Cait*, in honor of Śitala, goddess of smallpox (see Chapter XIV)
Somvārī amāvasyā: when the moonless night falls on a Monday; a fast
Somvarī pīlal: see *Somvārī amāvasyā*
sudī: the bright half of the lunar month
suhāgrāt: nuptial night
Śukla paksh: the bright half of the lunar month
syāhī: porcupine
ṭhaṅḍhāī: a drink made with milk, sugar, almonds, etc., usually with *bhāṅg* mixed in it
ṭhiṅguriyāṅ-moṅgariyāṅ: twigs and small branches
Tīj: a festival, observed on the third day of the bright half of *Sāvan*, in honor of Goddess Parvati (see Chapter III)
tilak: a colored mark on the forehead
tilkuṭ: sweet balls prepared with sesame seeds
tithī: lunar days
ṭonahinī: enchantress
tulsī: a sacred plant, grown in almost every Hindu household, whose leaves are used in ceremonies
Turkin: a Muslim woman
Turklin Pūjā: see Chapter VII
ubṭan: a paste made of flour, mustard oil, turmeric and water, used ro rub the body clean
Vaṭ Sāvitrī: see *Baragadāhī*
Vikram Samvat: the Hindu lunar calendar
vrat: fast
Yamdūt: the messenger of Yam

BIBLIOGRAPHY

Aarne, Antti. 1964. *The Types of the Folktale: A Classification and Bibliography*. Helsinki: Suomalainen Tiedeakatemia, Academia Scientiarum Fennica.

Ayer, V.A.K. 1975. *Untold Stories of King Bhoja*. Bombay: Bharatiya Vidya Bhavan.

Babb, Lawrence A. 1975. *The Divine Hierarchy: Popular Hinduism in Central India*. New York: Columbia University Press.

Bahadur, K.P. 1972. *Folk Tales of Uttar Pradesh*. New Delhi: Sterling Publishers.

Bareh, Hamlet. 1971. *Khasi Fables and Folk-Tales*. Calcutta: Firma K.L. Mukhopadhyay.

Bedi, Sohinder Singh. 1971. *Folklore of Punjab*. New Delhi: National Book Trust.

Bharatiya, Rupkishore and K.R. Brahmacari. 1974. *Barahon Mahine ke Sampurna Vrat aur Tauhar*. Mathura: Govardhan Pustakalaya.

Briggs, Geo. W. 1920. *The Chamars*. London: Oxford University Press.

Buch, C.H. 1917. *Faiths, Fairs, and Festivals of India*. Calcutta: Thacker, Spink & Co.

Buck William. 1973. *Mahabharata*. Berkeley, University of California Press.

——. 1978. *Ramayana: King Rama's Way*. New York: New American Library.

Buhler, Gerg (tr.). 1969. *The Laws of Manu*. New York: Dover Publications, Inc.

Chauhan, Brij Raj. 1967. *A Rajasthan Village*, New Delhi: Associated Publishing House.

Crooke, W. 1896. *The Popular Religion and Folklore of Northern India*. 2 vols. Delhi: Munshiram Manoharlal.

Devee, Maharanee Sunity. 1919. *Nine Ideal Indian Women*. Calcutta: Thacker, Spink & Co.

Dimmitt, Carnelia and J.A.B. van Buitenen. 1978. *Classical Hindu Mythology: A Reader in the Sanskrit Puranas*. Philadelphia: Temple University Press.

Dube, S.C. 1955. *Indian Village*. London: Routledge and Kegan Paul.

Elwin, Verrier. 1944. *Folk Tales of Mahakoshal*. London: Oxford University Press.

Frere, Mary. 1868. *Old Deccan Days*. London: John Murray.

Gargi Balwant. 1966. *Folk Theater of India*. Seattle: University of Washington Press.

Gautam, Chammanlal. 1975. *Vrata aur Tyohar*. Bareilly: Sanskrit Samsthana.

Gupte, B.A. Rai Bahadur. 1919. *Hindu Holidays and Ceremonials*. Calcutta: Thacker, Spink & Co.

Hein, Morvin. 1972. *The Miracle Plays of Mathura*. New Haven: Yale University Press.

Jacobson, Doranne. 1978. "The Chaste Wife: Cultural Norm and Individual Experience," *American Studies in the Anthropology of India*, ed. by Sylvia Vatuk, New Delhi: Manohar.

Khare, R.S. 1976. *The Hindu Hearth and Home*. New Delhi: Vikas Publishing House.

Kirkland, Edwin Capers. 1966. *A Bibliography of South Asian Folklore*. Bloomington: Indiana University Research Center in Anthropology, Folklore, and Linguistics.

Kothare, Balaji Sitaram. 1904. *Hindu Holidays*. Bombay: The Times Press.

Kuldeep. 1972. *Lok-Geeton ka Vikasatmaka Adhyayana*. Agra: Pragati Prakasana.

Kurrien, Zakiya (et al.). n.d. *Film Guide: An Indian Pilgrimage, Ramdevra*. Wisconsin: South Asian Area Center, University of Wisconsin.

Lall, R. Manohar. 1933. *Among the Hindus: A Study of Hindu Festivals*. Cawnpore: Minerva Press.

Lewis, Oscar. 1965. *Village Life in Northern India*. New York, Vintage Books.

Luschinsky, Mildred Stroop. 1962. "The Life of Women in a Village of North India: A Survey of Role and Status," unpublished Ph.D. dissertation, Cornell University.

Majumdar, Geeta. 1971. *Folk Tales of Bengal*. New Delhi: Sterling Publishers.

Mani, Vettam. 1979. *Puranic Encyclopaedia: A Comprehensive Dictionary with Special Reference to the Epic and Puranic Literature*. Delhi: Motilal Banarasi Dass.

Marriott, McKim. 1955. "Little Communities in an Indigenous Civilization," *Village India,* ed. by McKim Marriott. Chicago: University of Chicago Press.

Marzac, Nicole. 1977. "A Polish Version of A.T. 780 in Living Oral Tradition," *Ethnomusicology* 21(3): 397–413.

Mathur, K.S. 1964. *Caste and Ritual in a Malwa Village*. Bombay: Asia Publishing House.

Michael, S.M. 1983. "The Origin of the Ganapati Cult," *Asian Folklore Studies* 42(1): 91–116.

Mohanti, Prafulla. 1975. *Indian Village Tales*. London: Davis-Poynter.

Natesa Sastri, S.M. 1917. *Hindu Feasts, Fasts and Ceremonies*. Madras: M.E. Publishing House.

Nivedita, Sister. 1975. *Cradle Tales of Hinduism*. Calcutta: Advaita Ashrama.

North Indian Notes and Queries.

Pandey, Indu Prakash. 1967. *Avadhi Vrata-Kathayen*. New Delhi: Bharatiya Jnanpith.

Parmar, Shyam, 1969. *Malavi Lok-Sahitya*. Allahabad: Hindustani Academy.

———. 1975. *Madhya Pradesh: Lok Sanskrit aur Sahitya*. New Delhi: National Book Trust.

Pritchett, Frances W. 1982. "Preserving Ephemera: Chicago's Popular Literature Collection," *South Asia Library Notes and Queries* (11–12): 4–6.

Radhakrishnan. 1927. *The Hindu View of Life*. London: Unwin Books.

Ross, E. Denison (ed.). 1914. *An Alphabetical List of the Feasts and Holidays of the Hindus and Muhammadans*. Calcutta: Imperial Record Department.

Roy-Chaudhury, P.C. 1976. *Folklore of Bihar*. New Delhi: National Book Trust.

Ryder, Arthur W. 1956. *The Panchatantra*. Chicago: University of Chicago Press.

Sastri, Acarya Vagisha (ed.). 1975. *Asali Brahat Brahaspativar Vrat Katha*. Kanpur: Sri Krishna Pustakalaya.

Satyendra. 1957. *Brajloka Sahitya ka Adhyayana*. Agra: Sahitya-Ratna Bhandar.

———. 1962. *Loka Sahitya Vijnan*. Agra: Shivlal Agarwal & Co.

Shah, Ahmad. 1977. *The Bijak of Kabir.* New Delhi: Asia Publication Services.

Sharma, Shyamlal (ed.). 1972. *Dogari Lok Kathayen.* Jammu: Lalitkala, Sanskrit and Sahitya Academy.

Sinha, D.M. (Gen. ed.). 1976. *Census of India 1971: Series 21, Uttar Pradesh, Ethnographic Notes.* Lucknow: Director of Census Operations.

Sita. 1970. *Banaile Phool: Vraton aur Parvon ki Kathayen.* Delhi: National Publishing House.

Sivananda Swami. 1947. *Hindu Fasts and Festivals and their Philosophy.* Rishikesh: The Sivananda Publication League.

Tandon, Prakash. 1972. *Punjabi Century.* Delhi: Hind Pocket Books.

Tewari, Laxmi G. 1974. "Folk Music of India: Uttar Pradesh," unpublished Ph.D. dissertation, Wesleyan University, Connecticut.

———. 1977. "Ceremonial Songs of the Kanyakubja Brahmans," *Essays in Arts and Sciences* 6(1): 30-52.

———. 1978. *The Role of Folk Music in Socio-Educational Institutions,* paper read at the Xth International Congress of Anthropological and Ethnological Sciences in New Delhi, India, December 10–16.

Thomas, P. 1971. *Festivals and Holidays of India.* Bombay: D.B. Taraporevala.

Thompson, Stith. 1955-57. *Motif-Index of Folk-literature. A Classification of Narrative Elements in Folktales, Ballads, Myths, Fables, Medieval Romances, Exempla, Fabliaux, Jest-books, and Local Legends.* 5 vols. Bloomington: Indiana University Press.

Thompson, Stith and Warren E. Roberts. 1960. *Types of Indic Oral Tales: India, Pakistan and Ceylon.* Helsinki: Suomalainen Tiedeakatemia, Academia Scientiarum Fennica.

Thompson, Stith and Jonas Balys. 1976. *The Oral Tales of India.* Connecticut: Greenwood Press.

Tripathi, Suresh Chandra. 1977. *Kanauji Lok Sahitya me Samaj ka Pratibimba.* Delhi: Rupayana Prakasana.

Underhill, Muriel M. 1921. *The Hindu Religious Year.* London: Oxford University Press.

U.S. Department of State. 1982. *India: Background Notes.* Washington, D.C.: Bureau of Public Affairs.

Vequaud, Yves. 1977. *Women Painters of Mithila.* London: Thames and Hudson.

Wadley, Susan S. 1975. *Shakti: Power in the Conceptual Structure of Karimpur Religion.* Chicago: Department of Anthropology, University of Chicago.

———. 1978. "Texts in Contexts: Oral Traditions and the Study of Religion in Karimpur," *American Studies in the Anthropology of India*, ed. by. Sylvia Vatuk. New Delhi: Manohar.

———. 1978a. "Collecting Popular Traditions," *South Asia Library Notes and Queries* (1): 4–6.

Wiser, William H. and C.V. Wiser. 1971. *Behind Mud Walls.* Berkeley: University of California Press.

Zimmer, Heinrich. 1972. *Myths and Symbols in Indian Art and Civilization,* ed. by Joseph Campbell. Bollingen Foundation Series 6. New Jersey: Princeton University Press.

INDEX OF TALE TYPES

Arranged according to TR(= Thompson-Roberts, *Types of Indic Oral Tales: India, Pakistan and Ceylon*) and AT (= Aarne-Thompson, *The Types of the Folktales*).

TR Number	*AT Number*	*Story Number*
131	131	9, 9a
459	459	43, 43a
461B	461A	1
707	707	54
	750*	44
	778	45, 45a, 45b
780	780	40
897	897	32
910Z.2		30
923	923	28
1211	1211	10a
1333	1333	9, 54
	1373A	35, 35a

INDEX OF MOTIFS

Arranged according to TB (= Thompson-Balys, *The Oral Tales of India*) and Thompson, *Motif-Index of Folk-Literature*.

TB/Thompson	*Story Number*
A125.	1
A131.2	39, 42
A162	25, 53
A163	53
A181	50
A182	4, 39, 43, 45a, 49, 50, 52a, 54
A185.11	18, 20, 39
A287	25
A478.2	52
A487	4, 19, 26
A2493.24	9
B211.1.5	9, 9a
B211.1.5.2	10, 10a
B211.2.2	9, 9a, 28
B211.3	32, 41, 47a, 55
B211.3.7	32
B211.6.1	6, 6a, 7, 8, 28, 32, 38, 43a
B216	6, 7, 8, 10, 10a, 28, 32, 43a, 55
B225.1.1	7
B451.7	32
B457.2	32
B469.2	32
B491.1	6, 32, 38, 43a
B579.5	32
B656.2	43a
B765.6	28
C68	45, 45a
C319.1	43
C420.1	30
C611	6, 6a
C611.1	31
C900	15, 26, 35, 35a
C920.1	16, 16a, 20
C932	37

Contd.

TB/Thompson	*Story Number*
D141	12, 29
D391	7, 8, 38
D451.4.0.1	39
D454.8.1.1	8
D475.1	51, 54
D475.1.16	1
D476.2	1
D921.4	2
D1171.1	49
D1316.5.1	40
D1355.3	23, 23a
D1413.6	1
D1454.5	44
D1542.3.5	14, 14a
D1610.2	40, 52a
D1610.35	28, 50
D1766.8	55
D1766.10	21
D1810.0.3	21
D1867.1	1
D2087.7.1	1
D2161.4.14	2
E1	4, 11, 14, 14a, 17, 24, 37, 42, 42a, 43a
E29.4.1	40
E113	36
E121.1.2	16, 16a
E155.4	45a
E175	4
E613	20
E614.1	6
E631	40
E761.4.9.1	30
F953	2
F1034.3.1	32
H175.1	54
H430	47, 47a
H431.2	47a
H433.1	47a
H495.2	51
H592.1	28
H943.2	32
H1023.2	32
H1023.6	32
H1023.19	32
H1091.2	32

Contd.

TB/Thompson	*Story Number*
J21.22	30
J1111.6	43
J1701	11, 13
J1813	23, 23a, 27, 28, 33
J1835	10a
J2172.1	9
J2199.1.2	54
J2411	39
J2460	13
J2465	11
K1811	44, 49
K1811.2	16a
K2115.2.1	54
K2213	54
M20	8
M115.1	9a
M183	2
M300	52, 52a
M341.2.21	27
M359.5	2
N788	16a
N817	8, 25
N817.0.2	20, 43, 54
N831.1	36
N851	46
P253.0.5	37
P253.8	27, 27a, 28, 30
P253.10	28, 29, 31, 32, 33, 37
P273	34, 38
P274	34
P283	6
Q1.1	44
Q20.1	36, 52a
Q21	24,48
Q22	1, 5, 15, 22, 47, 51, 54
Q26	11, 12, 14, 14a, 16, 16a, 17, 18, 20, 37, 42a
Q28	1
Q45	52
Q83.1	4
Q111.2	44
O115.2	4
Q195	45a
Q221	18

Contd.

Contd.

TB/Thompson	*Story Number*
V1.8.6	6, 6a, 8
V12.4.5	45
V17.7	45
V85	1
V223.6	4, 5, 36, 52
W125.2	35, 35a
W157	35, 35a
Z71.1	4, 9a, 10, 19
Z71.5	6a, 20, 28, 33, 37, 43, 45a, 52, 52a, 54
Z71.5.1	32
Z71.8	2, 5, 36, 42a, 47a, 48, 50, 52
Z111.6	19, 27